GOD NEVER GIVES UP ON YOU

WHAT JACOB'S STORY TEACHES US ABOUT GRACE,
MERCY, AND GOD'S RELENTLESS LOVE

BIBLE STUDY GUIDE | FIVE SESSIONS

MAX LUCADO

WITH ANDREA L. RAMSAY

HarperChristian
Resources

CONTENTS

A NOTE FROM MAX LUCADO

You can't help but root for Jacob. His grandfather, Abraham, was the father of our faith, and from the beginning it is apparent that God has great plans for his life. But as you begin to read Jacob's story, you quickly find that he is a less-than-perfect figure. His journey seems to be two steps forward and one step back. He does something foolish, then he redevotes himself to God. Then he does something even more foolish and later remembers God again. You think he will arrive—that he will have an epiphany that changes him for good. But it never happens.

So, why does the Bible include Jacob's story at all? Perhaps because the point of Jacob's story is not Jacob. It is *God*. Throughout Jacob's trials, God remains faithful to him. He does not abandon him even on his darkest night or after his greatest mistake. God proves through Jacob's life that no matter what we do, no matter how many steps backward we take, he is always with us. The grace he gives us through his Son, Jesus, is greater than our biggest setback.

Jacob's story reveals that when we doubt our legacy—when we feel like the crooked bough on the family tree—God's grace will never fail us. His grace is the grand marshal of the parade, leading his ever-swelling cast of has-beens and never-weres out of halfway houses and prisons and into his palace. God's grace isn't only as good as we are—his grace is as good as *he* is. And it's not something that God gave just one time to people long ago. No, God's grace is given today . . . to anyone who will so much as call out to him in prayer.

God lowers the ladder to us. We do not have to climb it to him. When we run away, he stays. When we're foolish, he forgives. Perhaps no other character in Scripture proves this to be true of God more than Jacob. So, if you learn only one thing from this study, I hope it is this: God's grace never quits. He did not give up on Jacob. He will never give up on you.

— MAX LUCADO

How to Use This Guide

If you are a super saint, this study is not for you. If your faith never wavers, your Bible never closes, and your feet never stray, you won't relate to anything we will be covering. But if you're a member of the Tilted Halo Society—the fumblers and bumblers among us who are part saint and part scoundrel—you are going to love the story of Jacob.

Jacob was, by definition, a *patriarch*. When we think of the term, we think of stalwarts of the faith like Abraham, the father of the Jewish people. Sure, he had his failings, but he was called a friend of God (see Isaiah 41:8) and his faith was credited to him as righteousness (see Genesis 15:6). Or we think of Isaac, who carried on his father's faith in God. But when we come to Jacob, he seems less prodigy and more prodigal. Time and again, as you will see in this study, he was prone to wandering and misbehavior. But time and again, as you will also see, God chose to extend his grace to him. He never gave up on Jacob.

Before you begin, keep in mind that there are a few ways you can go through the material. You can experience the study with others in a group (such as a Bible study, Sunday school class, or any other small-group gathering), or you may choose to study the content on your own. Either way, the videos for each session are available for you to view at any time via streaming.

Group Study

Each session is divided into two parts: (1) a group study section and (2) a personal study section. The group study section is intended to provide a basic framework on how to open your time together, get the most out of the video content, and discuss the key ideas together that were presented in the teaching. Each session includes the following:

- **Welcome:** A short note about the topic of the session for you to read on your own before you meet together as a group.
- **Connect:** A few icebreaker questions to get you and your group members thinking about the topic and interacting with one another.

- **Watch:** An outline of the key points that will be covered in each video teaching to help you follow along, stay engaged, and take notes.
- **Discuss:** Questions to help your group reflect on the teaching material presented and apply it to your lives.
- **Respond:** A short personal exercise to help reinforce the key ideas.
- **Pray:** A place for you to record prayer requests and praises for the week.

If you are doing this study in a group, make sure you have your own copy of this study guide so you can write down your thoughts, responses, and reflections and have access to the videos via streaming. You will also want to have a copy of the *God Never Gives Up on You* book, as reading it alongside the curriculum will provide you with deeper insights. (See the notes at the start of each group session and personal study section on which chapters you should read before the next group session.)

Finally, keep these points in mind:

- **Facilitation:** If you are doing this study in a group, you will want to appoint someone to serve as a facilitator. This person will be responsible for starting the video and keeping track of time during discussions and activities. If *you* have been chosen for this role, there are some resources in the back of this guide that can help you lead your group through the study.

- **Faithfulness:** Your small group is a place where tremendous growth can happen as you reflect on the Bible, ask questions, and learn what God is doing in other people's lives. For this reason, be fully committed and attend each session so you can build trust and rapport with the other members.

- **Friendship:** The goal of any small group is to serve as a place where people can share, learn about God, and build friendships. So seek to make your group a "safe place." Be honest about your thoughts and feelings . . . but also listen carefully to everyone else's thoughts, feelings, and opinions. Keep anything personal that your group members share in confidence so that you can create a community where people can heal, be challenged, and grow spiritually.

If you are studying on your own, read the opening Welcome section and reflect on the questions in the Connect section. Watch the video and use the outline provided to take notes. Finally, personalize the questions and exercises in the Discuss and Respond sections. Close by recording any requests you want to pray about during the week.

Personal Study

The personal study is for you to experience on your own during the week. Each exercise is designed to help you explore the key ideas you uncovered during your group time and delve into passages of Scripture that will help you apply those principles to your life. Go at your own pace, doing a little each day or all at once, and spend a few moments in silence to listen to what God might be saying to you. Each personal study includes:

- **Open:** A brief introduction to lead you into the personal study for the day.
- **Read:** A few passages on the topic of the day for you to read and review.
- **Reflect:** Questions for you to answer related to the passages you just read.
- **Pray:** A prompt to help you express what you've studied in a prayer to God.

If you are doing this study as part of a small group, and you are unable to finish (or even start) these personal studies for the week, you should still attend the group time. Be assured that you are still wanted and welcome even if you don't have your "homework" done. The group studies and personal studies are intended to help you hear what the Lord wants you to hear and apply what he is saying to your life. So be listening for him to speak to you as you learn about what it means that God never gives up on you.

Schedule

WEEK 1

BEFORE GROUP MEETING	Read chapters 1–3 of *God Never Gives Up on You* Read the Welcome section (page 3)
GROUP MEETING	Discuss the Connect questions Watch the video teaching for session 1 Discuss the questions that follow as a group Do the closing exercise and pray (pages 3–10)
PERSONAL STUDY – DAY 1	Complete the daily study (pages 13–14)
PERSONAL STUDY – DAY 2	Complete the daily study (pages 15–16)
PERSONAL STUDY – DAY 3	Complete the daily study (pages 17–18)
PERSONAL STUDY – DAY 4	Complete the daily study (pages 19–20)
CATCH UP & READ AHEAD - DAY 5 (before week 2 group meeting)	Read chapters 4–5 of *God Never Gives Up on You* Complete any unfinished personal studies

TAKING SHORTCUTS

The revelation awaits an appointed time;
it speaks of the end and will not prove false.
Though it linger, wait for it;
it will certainly come and will not delay.

HABAKKUK 2:3

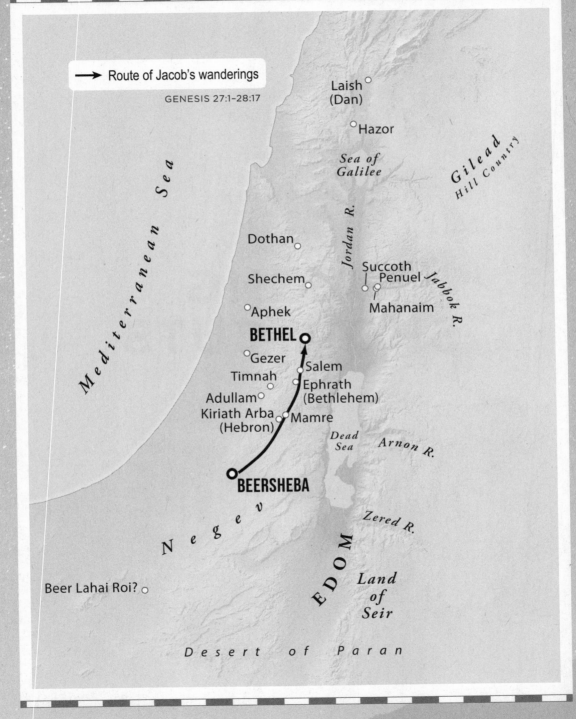

Route of Jacob's wanderings

GENESIS 27:1–28:17

Laish (Dan)

Hazor

Sea of Galilee

Gilead Hill Country

Jordan R.

Dothan

Shechem

Succoth

Penuel

Jabbok R.

Mahanaim

Aphek

BETHEL

Gezer

Salem

Timnah

Ephrath (Bethlehem)

Adullam

Kiriath Arba (Hebron)

Mamre

Dead Sea

Arnon R.

BEERSHEBA

N e g e v

Zered R.

Mediterranean Sea

E D O M

Land of Seir

Beer Lahai Roi?

D e s e r t   o f   P a r a n

Welcome |

No family is perfect. Even the best ones have branches of the family tree that go rogue. When you consider your own family, you can surely think of an aunt or great-grandfather that was a black sheep or left a less-than-perfect legacy. We find families like this in the Bible as well. Yes, even biblical families had their problems and their problem-causing characters! Humans are all broken, and these ancient families were no exception.

Jacob is a perfect example of a member of a great family who left a less-than-perfect legacy. He had a reputation for taking shortcuts. Before he was born, God promised that he would be a leader of a great nation (see Genesis 25:23). But instead of waiting for God to fulfill the promise, Jacob (with the help of his mother, Rebekah) took matters into his own hands. He strategized to secure his brother's birthright and then outright stole his brother's blessing. Rather than waiting, he took. Rather than asking God to make a way, he made a way for himself. The story didn't end well.

Shortcuts are tempting. God does not operate on our preferred timelines, so when we see an opportunity to take matters into our hands, we often do. But there is a reason why God calls us to wait—and there are consequences for not waiting. In particular, as we will see in this first session, when we fail to trust in God's promises and try to rush his timeline, we typically only end up bringing misery on ourselves and on the people we love.

Connect | 15 MINUTES

If you or any of your group members don't know each other, take a few minutes to introduce yourselves. Then, to get things started, discuss one of the following questions:

• Why did you decide to join this study? What do you hope to learn?

— *or* —

• When you think about your family's legacy, who or what sticks out to you?

Watch | 20 MINUTES

Now watch the video for this session, which you can access by playing the DVD or through streaming (see the instructions provided with this guide). Below is an outline of the key points covered during the teaching. Record any thoughts or concepts that stand out to you.

Outline

I. Sturdy oaks and crooked trees

    A. Some family members are remembered like the sturdy oaks and majestic sequoias. They leave behind a powerful legacy with their words, works, and actions.

    B. Others leave behind a legacy that is a bit more *crooked*. The events they encounter in life cause them to cave and compromise. We see this in the family tree of Abraham.

    C. Abraham was wealthy in herds, flocks, silver, and gold. He was also affluent in faith. His son Isaac was born to him and his wife, Sarah, in their old age. Isaac married Rebekah, and their sons were Esau and Jacob.

II. The birthright and the blessing

    A. Esau means "hairy" in Hebrew. He was manly, ruddy . . . and hairy. Jacob means "he grasps the heel," so named because he grasped Esau's heel during birth. He would grow into a real heel.

    B. Jacob liked shortcuts. One day when Esau came home from hunting without any snacks, Jacob convinced his elder brother to trade his birthright for a bowl of stew.

    C. Jacob even stepped into Esau's name and hobby. He dressed up like Esau, cooked his elderly father a meal, and duped Isaac into giving him the blessing that belonged to Esau.

    D. When Esau found out about Jacob's duplicity, the hunter decided it was time for a new type of prey. He said in his heart, "I will kill my brother Jacob" (Genesis 27:41 NKJV). Jacob fled.

III. The cost of a burgled blessing

    A. Jacob's family was splintered and he was now living a life on the run. He had betrayed his father's trust and, as far as we know, he never saw his mother again.

    B. Jacob's life became a mare's nest of misery. The day after running away from home, he was sleeping on the ground with a rock for a pillow. All because he took a shortcut.

    C. Jacob was a liar, a cheat, a thief, and a deceiver. He was a crooked tree in the family line. But he was also beloved of God. He was precious in God's sight.

IV. A vision and a promise

    A. Jacob had a dream in the wilderness of a ladder that "reached to heaven; and there the angels of God were ascending and descending on it" (Genesis 28:12 NKJV).

    B. Jacob's vision didn't end with the ladder. The Lord of heaven said, "I am with you and will keep you wherever you go, and will bring you back to this land" (Genesis 28:15 NKJV).

C. At Jacob's lowest moment—alone, abandoned, and afraid—God chose to cover him with grace. The Lord loved Jacob in spite of all his faults.

V. God's stubborn refusal to give up on you

   A. God is present with you. He is speaking to you. He is inviting you to look up and lean into him.

   B. Your ladder into heaven is not a vision. Yours is a person. Jesus is your stairway.

   C. Jesus is at both ends of the ladder. He is the conduit through which blessings come and prayers ascend. He is the intermediary between you and God.

   D. The promise in Jacob's story is that God is in the wilderness, in the despair, in the misery, in the mess and mayhem, and in the broken hearts.

Discuss | 35 MINUTES

Discuss what you just watched by answering the following questions. There are some suggested questions below to help you begin your discussion, but feel free to pick any of the additional questions as time allows.

Suggested Questions

1. At one point during Rebekah's pregnancy, she asked the Lord about why the two babies "jostled each other within her" (Genesis 25:22). Read God's reply in Genesis 25:23. How might this prophecy have affected Rebekah and Jacob's future actions?

2. The Bible reveals that Jacob was impatient and often took shortcuts. How did he scheme with his mother, Rebekah, to deceive his father, Isaac? What did Jacob receive from Isaac as a result? What were the consequences of their actions?

3. It's easy to fault Jacob for his foolishness. But what about you? When have you taken a shortcut because you grew impatient with waiting on God? What happened in that situation as a result of your impatience?

4. Read Genesis 28:10–15. At Jacob's lowest moment, God chose to appear to him and cover him with his grace. What does this say about how God felt toward Jacob? What does this say about how God feels about us, even when we take shortcuts?

Additional Questions

5. Read Genesis 28:16–17. How did Jacob's dream change the way he viewed God? When is a time that you suddenly became aware of God's presence in your life like this?

6. The apostle Paul writes, "There is one God and one mediator between God and mankind, the man Christ Jesus" (1 Timothy 2:5). How is Jesus our "ladder" to God?

7. If God were to call down to you from the ladder just as he did with Jacob, what would you want to hear him say to you?

8. What is the promise for each of us in Jacob's story? How could you find strength in that promise today?

Respond | 10 MINUTES

Sketch out your perception of your family tree. Draw sturdy branches, crooked branches, small branches—whatever represents your family. For your branch, draw the type of legacy that you *hope* to leave. When you are finished, share your sketch with the group.

Pray | 10 MINUTES

Praying for one another is one of the most important things you can do as a community. So use this time wisely and make it more than just a "closing prayer" to end your group experience. Be intentional about sharing your prayers, reviewing how God is answering them, and actually praying as a group. Use the space below to write down any requests so that you and your group members can continue to pray about them in the week ahead.

Name	Request

PERSONAL STUDY

The story of Jacob, the "crooked" patriach in the Bible, offers a wealth of truths that you can apply to your own life. A key part of uncovering these truths is studying Scripture. This is the goal of these personal studies—to help you explore what the Bible has to say and apply what you are reading in Jacob's story to your life. As you work through each of these exercises, be sure to write down your responses to the questions, as you will be given a few minutes to share your insights at the start of the next session (if you are doing this study with others). If you are reading *God Never Gives Up on You* alongside this study, first read chapters 1–2.

Day 1
FAITH OVER FEAR

Before Jacob was born, God revealed to his mother, Rebekah, what his future would hold: "One people will be stronger than the other, and the older will serve the younger" (Genesis 25:23). Rebekah remembered these powerful words from God, and it is likely that she told them to Jacob. The two worked together to secure Isaac's blessing for Jacob and make the prophecy come true.

But is this what God intended? When the Lord revealed the brothers' destinies to Rebekah, it was in response to her prayer: "The babies jostled each other within her, and she said, 'Why is this happening to me?' So she went to inquire of the LORD" (Genesis 25:22). Her response, and Jacob's response, was not trust. It was instead an effort to take matters into their own hands—to "help" God in making sure that the prophecy came true.

Why didn't Rebekah and Jacob simply trust God? While the Bible doesn't say for sure, we can assume it is because *trusting God is hard*. It's far easier to respond in *fear*. Fear that the words won't come to fruition. Fear that we will miss out on a blessing unless we do something about it. Fear that God's timing is all wrong. Prophetic words can be a blessing when we respond to them in trust, but they can be a curse when we respond to them in fear.

Think about the words that have been spoken over you in your life. Maybe these were words from a minister, a family member, or a friend. How did you respond? Did you feel pressure to fulfill them? Did you set your sights on them and nothing else? Did you feel disappointed when they weren't fulfilled in the *way* you thought they would be or *when* you thought they would be?

Prophecy is a delicate spiritual act. Today, you will read about the prophecies given to two other individuals in the Bible—Abraham and Mary—and see how their responses differed from Rebekah's and Jacob's. As you read about these recipients of God's word, think about what happens when you respond to God in *faith* rather than out of *fear*.

READ | GENESIS 12:1–4 AND LUKE 1:30–38

REFLECT

1. The story of Abram (later known as Abraham) begins with an account of his father, Terah, moving the family from Ur of the Chaldeans to Harran (see Genesis 11:27–32), a distance of approximately 600 miles. What sacrifice did God then ask Abram to make to fulfill the plans he had for him? What was Abram's response?

2. Mary was an unmarried virgin when the angel Gabriel appeared to her with the calling of a lifetime. How did Mary respond to this call (see Luke 1:38)? What sacrifice do you think this required on her part to respond to the angel in this way?

3. What are some of the ways you have sensed God calling you or leading you at various points in your life? How did you respond to these promptings from God?

4. What is something you are facing right now that you're tempted to react or respond to out of fear? How could you choose trust and obedience instead?

PRAY | End your time in prayer. Consider how you have responded to God's voice in the past. Ask him to help you respond to him in faith, obedience, and trust.

Day 2
VICTIMS OF SHORTCUTS

Rebekah and Jacob were not the first in their family line to try and secure God's promises through their own efforts. Abraham and Sarah were the first to set this trend. The Bible reveals that God made a covenant with Abraham, promising, "'A son who is your own flesh and blood will be your heir.' He took him outside and said, 'Look up at the sky and count the stars—if indeed you can count them.' Then he said to him, 'So shall your offspring be'" (Genesis 15:4–5).

It was an incredible promise from God. But there was just one problem: Abraham and Sarah were old. Their childbearing years were long behind them. It was hard for them to believe how this promise could ever come to pass. So Sarah (first known as Sarai) took matters into her own hands. "Now Sarai . . . had an Egyptian slave named Hagar; so she said to Abram, 'The LORD has kept me from having children. Go, sleep with my slave; perhaps I can build a family through her'" (Genesis 16:1–2). Abraham agreed, and eventually Hagar gave birth to Ishmael.

However, this was not God's plan for Abraham and Sarah, and the couple would soon reap the consequences for taking shortcuts. Hagar "began to despise her mistress" (verse 4). Sarah, in turn, grew disdainful of Hagar and mistreated her to the point that Hagar fled from her (see verse 6). Later, she was cast out of the community by Sarah (see Genesis 21:10).

Because of Sarah's shortcut, an innocent woman and her son suffered greatly. While God took care of Hagar and Ishmael, they would not have endured this pain if Sarah hadn't taken her and Abraham's future into her own hands—and if Abraham hadn't agreed to the plan. Two generations later, Esau would suffer in a similar way at the hands of those attempting to "play God." He lost his birthright and blessing, the victim of a plan that wasn't God's.

This is the thing about taking matters into our own hands—in trying to protect ourselves, we can hurt others. And while God ultimately looks out for all his children, we must live with the consequences of our actions and the consequences they have on those around us.

READ | GENESIS 21:14–20

REFLECT

1. Hagar, being an enslaved woman, did not have rights and was considered the property of her mistress, Sarah.[1] She would have had no choice but to be Sarah's surrogate and do as she was told—and no choice when she was then cast out of the community alone, with her young son, and with no money or husband as her protector. According to this passage, how was Hagar feeling about her and her son's situation?

2. How did God respond to Hagar when he heard her son crying? Considering her position in life, how do you think it felt for her to hear God's words about the destiny of her son?

3. When have your actions negatively affected those around you?

4. Looking back, how could trusting or obeying God in that situation have prevented what happened to you and to those around you?

PRAY | Ask God to open your eyes to the Hagars in your community—the ones who are victims of their circumstances or someone else's actions. Ask the Lord to help you see those individuals as he sees them—his children whom he loves.

Day 3

JESUS AS OUR LADDER

Jacob's vision of a ladder can seem unrelatable to us today. After all, how many of us have seen something like that? A ladder descending from heaven with angels going up and down? The image is supernatural . . . something only the "holiest" saints have witnessed. But as we've seen, Jacob's ladder was not only a promise for Jacob. It's a promise for us as well.

The ladder in Jacob's vision connected him to God. In the same way, Jesus connects *us* to God. As he said of himself, "Truly, truly, I say to you, you will see heaven opened, and the angels of God ascending and descending on the Son of Man" (John 1:51 ESV). Jesus also refers to himself as the "Son of Man" eighty-two times in Scripture—a reference that likely relates to a prophecy in Daniel 7:13–14). The name is meant to point to Christ's divine nature.

We are not divine like God. So Jesus bridges the human-divine divide for us. He reveals God's nature to us. If we want to know what God is like, we look at Jesus. If we want to know how God feels about us, we look at how Jesus felt about others. Jesus makes God relatable and allows us a direct line to God's throne room. Our prayers don't float up into nowhere. We have an intercessor in Jesus, speaking with God on our behalf. And, the greatest news of all, this intercessor vouches for us. He took on our sin so that we could spend eternity with God—not separated from the divine but fully present with him for all eternity.

The next time you feel misunderstood, or unheard, or like you messed up one too many times and God could never forgive you, just remember that *Jesus is your ladder*. It's not up to you to get to God. It's Jesus' job, and he is always there reaching out his hand to you.

READ | HEBREWS 7:23–28 AND ROMANS 8:34–39

REFLECT

1. A high priest in Old Testament times was the ultimate spiritual leader for the Jewish people. One of his roles was to enter an area of the temple known as the Holy of Holies on Yom Kippur, the Day of Atonement, and make a sacrifice on behalf of the sins of the people. The presence of God resided in the Holy of Holies, so only the high priest was allowed to enter, and only one time each year. As you consider this context, what does it mean when the author of Hebrews says that Jesus is our high priest?

2. According to Paul, what does Jesus do for us that we cannot do for ourselves? How should this impact the way we view God and approach him?

3. Has anyone in your life ever interceded for you, vouched for you, or defended you? If so, what was that experience like for you?

4. How have you experienced Jesus as your high priest or your intercessor? Or, is it difficult for you to view Jesus in this way? Explain your response.

PRAY | Come today before Jesus, your great high priest. What do you need? What are you grateful for? What are you worried about? What do you hope for? Bring all your prayers and thoughts to him and trust that he is interceding to the Father on your behalf.

Day 4

THE GIFT OF GRACE

In every story, there is a *protagonist*—a character who serves as the hero of the tale. When we read Jacob's story in the Bible, we might be tempted to view him in this role. After all, it is a story about his life. But Jacob is not the hero of his own story. God is! God bestowed his grace on Jacob and appeared to him in a vision for no other reason than he loved Jacob and wanted to reassure him of his presence. The initiator of grace was God—and God alone.

Jacob certainly didn't deserve the vision that God gave to him. He had just stolen his brother's blessing. He was running away from his mistakes to save his life. As far as we know, he hadn't experienced a change of heart. He hadn't apologized to Esau or made amends. While he likely felt afraid, we don't even know if he felt guilty or regretful. It's not that Jacob changed and so God decided to bless him. As one scholar notes, "There is no word of reproach for Jacob. God simply takes the initiative in extending grace to this schemer."[2]

This is also true in our stories. We haven't done anything—and actually *can't* do anything—to earn God's grace. No, we receive it as a free and unmerited gift—through Jesus, our ladder—simply because our heavenly Father loves us and wants us to know that he is always with us. We can't fall out of grace with God, and we are never beyond his mercy. His love is greater than anything we could ever do (or not do) in this life.

God gave Jacob a beautiful promise: "I am with you and will watch over you wherever you go, and I will bring you back to this land. I will not leave you until I have done what I have promised you" (Genesis 28:15). While we may feel distant from God at times because of what we have done, the truth is that God is never distant from us.

READ | LAMENTATIONS 3:22–24 AND EPHESIANS 2:4–8

REFLECT

1. True to its name, Lamentations is a book about lamenting, specifically the Israelites' lamenting that Jerusalem had been captured by the Babylonians in 587 BC. The Israelites had long strayed from God's plan, and the capture was seen as a punishment. Losing Jerusalem and the temple was equivalent to losing themselves, and the author of Lamentations (likely Jeremiah) expresses this anguish. But in Lamentations 3:22–24, the author changes his tune. What does he say about God's love and mercy? Why is this significant in the context of Israel's rebellion and capture by the Babylonians?

2. How does Paul describe our condition before we came to Christ? What has God done for us now that we are in Christ? What part do we play in this?

3. When is a time that you experienced God's grace and mercy in a tangible way? What was that experience like? How did it make you feel about God and yourself?

4. What area of your life have you been hiding from God's grace and mercy? What would it look like to receive his love in this part of your life rather than condemnation?

PRAY | Spend your prayer time in quiet reflection. Let yourself feel God's love, grace, and mercy. Pay attention to what it feels like in your heart, brain, and body. Stay in this moment for as long as you are able.

Day 5

CATCH UP & READ AHEAD

Use this time to go back and complete any study and reflection questions from previous days this week that you weren't able to finish. Make a note below of any revelations you've had and reflect on any growth or personal insights you've gained.

Spend the next two days reading chapters 4–5 of *God Never Gives Up on You*. Use the space below to record anything in the chapters that stands out to you or encourages you.

Schedule

WEEK 2

BEFORE GROUP MEETING	Read chapters 4–5 of *God Never Gives Up on You* Read the Welcome section (page 25)
GROUP MEETING	Discuss the Connect questions Watch the video teaching for session 2 Discuss the questions that follow as a group Do the closing exercise and pray (pages 25–32)
PERSONAL STUDY – DAY 1	Complete the daily study (pages 35–36)
PERSONAL STUDY – DAY 2	Complete the daily study (pages 37–38)
PERSONAL STUDY – DAY 3	Complete the daily study (pages 39–40)
PERSONAL STUDY – DAY 4	Complete the daily study (pages 41–42)
CATCH UP & READ AHEAD - DAY 5 (before week 3 group meeting)	Read chapters 6–7 of *God Never Gives Up on You* Complete any unfinished personal studies

REAPING WHAT YOU SOW

*As I have observed, those who plow evil
and those who sow trouble reap it.*

JOB 4:8

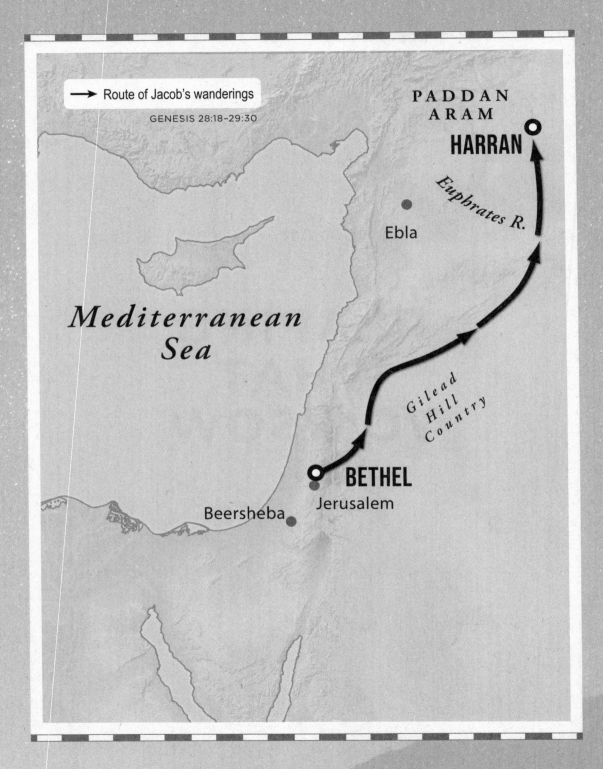

Route of Jacob's wanderings

GENESIS 28:18–29:30

PADDAN ARAM

HARRAN

Euphrates R.

Ebla

Mediterranean Sea

Gilead Hill Country

BETHEL

Jerusalem

Beersheba

Welcome | READ ON YOUR OWN

Gardening can be a rewarding experience. You put seeds in the ground at just the right time. You work hard to create an environment in which those seeds will thrive—rich soil, fertilizer, and plenty of sun and water. Once the buds start sprouting, you know that all your hard work has paid off. An abundance of squash, kale, and herbs awaits you.

But gardening is a less-than-rewarding experience if you neglect to do these things. If you don't pull up the weeds that can choke a plant, or if you don't water your garden, or even if you don't plant enough seeds in the first place, you will not witness an abundance. Instead, you will discover that "whoever sows sparingly will also reap sparingly" (2 Corinthians 9:6).

You've probably experienced this reality outside the context of a garden. You commit to chipping away at your job and are one day given a promotion. You put in the hard work of loving your child through the tough times and are rewarded with a thriving relationship. You study hard for a test and receive a good grade. Whatever you put into your life—whatever "seeds" you choose to sow—you will get out, whether it's good or bad.

As you saw in the last session, the seeds that Jacob sowed in his life were those of deception. He first tricked his brother, Esau, and then he fooled his father, Isaac. He sowed seeds of treachery. Now, in today's session, you will see the kind of harvest that would produce in his life. For Jacob was about to meet his match in deception in the form of an uncle named Laban.

Connect | 15 MINUTES

Get the session started by choosing one of these questions to discuss as a group:

- What is a key insight or takeaway from last week's personal study that you would like to share with the group?

— or —

- When have you bargained with God—*If you do this for me, I'll do this for you*? What ultimately was the result of your bargaining?

Watch | 20 MINUTES

Now watch the video for this session. Below is an outline of the key points covered during the teaching. Record any thoughts or concepts that stand out to you.

I. You will always reap what you sow.

   A. Whatever you plant into the soil is what is going to come out. Almonds grow from almond trees, walnuts from walnut trees, and dates from date palms.

   B. The same principle is true in life. In Jacob's case, the seeds he planted transformed him from prince to pauper, from beloved to bedraggled, from connected to cut off.

   C. Trees don't always "breed true." You may not get the same quality of fruit from the tree you are planting as from the tree the seed came from originally. You have to wonder if people were saying the same about Jacob.

D. Jacob was from the line of Abraham, a man who—in spite of his own flaws—had reaped the seeds of faithfulness to God and been rewarded with land and a promised son.

II. Jacob tries to make a deal with the divine.

A. At Jacob's lowest point, God made an appearance and promised to be with him wherever he went and to bring him back home (see Genesis 28:15).

B. But instead of receiving God's blessing and being grateful, Jacob hammered out the key points of a contract (see Genesis 28:20–21).

C. A working term for this arrangement is *transactional theology*. It presupposes that we meet God on equal terms—that we can make a deal with the Divine because we have something that God wants.

D. The result of transactional theology is disillusionment. We reduce God to a pocket-sized deity and miss out on having a life-giving relationship with him.

III. Jacob was about to learn that he could not bargain with God.

    A. Jacob set out for the land of Harran to meet his uncle, Laban, and find a wife. Once there, Jacob met a girl named Rachel at a well. She was the daughter of Jacob's uncle.

    B. Laban was on the varsity team when it came to swindling. Jacob agreed to work *seven* years—double the expected dowry—to marry Rachel (see Genesis 29:14–15).

    C. When the seven years had passed, Laban threw the wedding party as promised. But the next morning, Jacob was shocked to find beside him not Rachel but her older sister, Leah.

    D. Jacob planted seeds of deceit and harvested the crop of deceit. He should have learned his lesson. But Jacob remained stiff and unresponsive.

IV. Each of us fits into the story of Jacob.

    A. God sent Jacob multiple messages. Some of these messages came in the form of blessings, and some came in the form of burdens. God gave Jacob plenty of opportunities to learn his lessons and change his ways.

    B. It's incredible that Jacob never did. But what's even more incredible is that God never gave up on Jacob. Grace, grace, grace.

    C. How do we fit into this story? Before we blame Laban or scowl at Leah, we need to take a long look in the mirror. Jacob's story is a warning that we reap what we sow.

    D. What seeds are you sowing today? What kind of fruit do you want to see in your life? You determine the quality of tomorrow by the seeds you sow today.

Discuss | 35 MINUTES

Discuss what you just watched by answering the following questions. There are some suggested questions below to help you begin your discussion, but feel free to pick any of the additional questions as time allows.

Suggested Questions

1. Read Genesis 28:18–22. Jacob's response to God's vision is an example of what we can call *transactional theology*. Why do we so often operate in this way with God? How does transactional theology prevent us from experiencing a deep relationship with God?

2. Read Genesis 29:14–27. Consider how Laban's deception of Jacob parallels Jacob's deception of Esau and Isaac. How did Jacob reap what he sowed? Do we *always* reap what we sow, or have you experienced exceptions to this rule? Explain your answer.

3. What did Jacob learn from his experience with Laban? What have you learned from experiences where you've reaped what you sowed—whether the fruit was good or bad?

4. What kind of "seeds" do you believe you are sowing in your family, work, church, or community? What would it take to sow *good* seeds in all these places?

Additional Questions

5. Jacob was transactional in his relationship with God. He was saying that *if* God did certain things for him, *then* he would respond a certain way. What are some ways that you have been transactional in your relationship with God? What is the danger in believing that God is just a genie who will provide for everything you request?

6. Who has sown seeds of goodness in your life in which you are now seeing the fruit? What is that fruit, and how does this encourage you to sow goodness in others?

7. Consider how you now feel about Jacob after hearing this week's teaching. What are some areas in which you empathize with him? What frustrates you about him?

8. Paul writes, "It is by grace you have been saved, through faith—and this is not from yourselves, it is the gift of God" (Ephesians 2:8). Grace seems to be the antithesis to reaping what we sow—we get God's goodness instead of what we deserve. How do you reconcile this idea of God's free gift of grace with the idea that we reap what we sow?

Respond | 10 MINUTES

Paul writes that "the fruit of the Spirit is love, joy, peace, forbearance, kindness, goodness, faithfulness, gentleness and self-control" (Galatians 5:22–23). List any examples of this kind of fruit you've seen lately in your life and what might have been the "seed" or origin of how that fruit was planted. Share your responses with the group if you have time.

Pray | 10 MINUTES

End your time by praying together. Ask the Lord to help you sow good seeds this week in your life and in your work. Ask if anyone has any prayer requests. Write those requests in the space below so you and your group members can pray about them in the week ahead.

Name	Request

PERSONAL STUDY

We reap what we sow. This was the lesson that Jacob began to learn in the events we've covered this week, and it is our lesson to learn as well. We can sow seeds that lead either to consequences or to blessing. As you explore this theme in this week's personal study, be sure to write down your responses to the questions in the spaces provided, as you will be given a few minutes to share your insights at the start of the next session if you are doing this study with others. If you are reading *God Never Gives Up on You* while doing this study, read chapters 4–5.

Day 1

SEEDS AND SOIL

This week, we talked a lot about reaping and sowing. Sow good seeds and you get good fruit. But what is essential to growing healthy fruit? Healthy *soil*. While dirt is a lifeless mixture of minerals, air, and water, healthy soil is rich in organic matter and living organisms, like good bacteria and fungi, that allow the plant to thrive.[3] A plant is only as good as its soil.

Up to this point, Jacob had not cultivated good soil in his life. He had deceived his father and brother, and even when God gave him a vision and blessing at Bethel, he didn't seem to fully understand or appreciate it. By the time Jacob met Laban, it is quite possible the soil he had cultivated prevented him from discerning the deceiver in his conniving uncle. You could say that Jacob's soil was dry and lifeless *dirt* that was producing dry and lifeless fruit.

If we want to produce good fruit, we must first cultivate healthy soil. According to the apostle Paul, the fruit of the Spirit consists of traits such as "love, joy, peace, forbearance, kindness, goodness, faithfulness, gentleness and self-control" (Galatians 5:22–23). Often when we see this list, we think of these as traits for which to strive. *I must try to be patient. I must try to be loving. I must try to be gentle.* But how does all this trying and striving typically work out? We eventually lose our patience. We come across someone who is difficult to love. We snap and lash out at a coworker. Then we feel guilty for not trying hard enough.

Fruit cannot be forced. It can only be grown. And it can grow only in a healthy environment. Our job isn't to make ourselves kind and gentle. Our job is to create an environment in our lives that naturally cultivates the fruit of the Spirit to grow in us.

READ | Matthew 13:1–9, 18–23

REFLECT

1. This account in Matthew's Gospel is typically known as the parable of the sower. Jesus often spoke in parables that related to his largely agricultural audience in ancient Palestine. They understood the metaphors of seeds, sowing, and soil, for these were their livelihood. What types of soil does Jesus describe in this parable? What does each represent? What does the seed that the farmer scatters represent?

2. According to Jesus' words in verse 23 of the parable, what happens to the seed that falls in good soil? What does the large crop symbolize in the kingdom of God?

3. Based on the type of fruit you see in your life today, what kind of soil have you been cultivating? Explain your response.

4. What fruit do you *hope* to produce in your life? What could you do to improve your "soil" so that this kind of fruit can start to grow and flourish?

PRAY | For your prayer time, visualize your life as a field ready for harvest. What plants do you see? What fruit is growing? Ask God to show you what your heart is capable of producing. Ask him what you can do to make yourself more attentive to his voice and receptive to his message.

Day 2
BARGAINING WITH GOD

When God gave Jacob a vision at Bethel and promised to be with him and watch over him, the patriarch made what we might consider to be an odd response. He made a bargain with God: "If God will be with me and will watch over me on this journey I am taking and will give me food to eat and clothes to wear so that I return safely to my father's household, then the LORD will be my God and this stone that I have set up as a pillar will be God's house, and of all that you give me I will give you a tenth" (Genesis 28:20–22).

God had already made Jacob a promise, yet Jacob felt the need to test it. It's an instinct that we understand only too well. It's hard to trust God at his word. The future is unknown and uncertain. So we make an offer to God to try and "sweeten the deal" in case he changes his mind. *If you give me this promotion, then I'll pray every day. If you get me out of this mess, then I'll start tithing. If you restore that relationship, I will attend church more faithfully.*

This is often how we operate with people. We do someone a favor as long as that person does one for us in return. Rarely do we give altruistically with no expectations of getting anything out of the deal. But this is not how God works. He doesn't need our gifts or empty promises. He doesn't want our faith to be conditional based on what we get or don't get from him. He wants our unconditional devotion. This is, after all, what he has given us.

God gave us his Son with no strings attached. He offered us forgiveness from sin, expecting nothing in return. Grace is not conditional or transactional. We only get into trouble when we try to "bargain" with God, as the following story from Judges relates.

READ | JUDGES 11:30–39

REFLECT

1. Jephthah was an Israelite during the time of the judges who was put in charge of defeating a group called the Ammonites. However, he was uncertain of his calling, so he made a bargain with God to ensure his victory. It was common in ancient times to make deals with deities before battle—even deals that would require human sacrifice.[4] How did Jephthah react when he saw his daughter come out of the door of his house? How do you think he felt for the two months that she was wandering in the hills?

2. Because animals were not traditionally kept in the house during these times, Jephthah likely anticipated a friend or family member would be the first to come out of his house.[5] Why do you think Jephthah was willing to make such a bargain with God? What does his story teach us about the dark side of having a transactional relationship with God?

3. Have you ever made a bargain with God that you ended up not wanting to keep? What was the bargain and why was it difficult for you to hold up your end?

4. What would your relationship with God look like if it weren't transactional—if there were no vows, bargains, or promises made in exchange for what you want?

PRAY | End your time in prayer. Reflect on the bargains you've made with God in the past or one that you've recently made. What are you wanting God to do for you? How could you talk to God about this request in a way that doesn't include bargaining or transactions?

Day 3

PRAYING FOR WHAT GOD WANTS

You probably have many reasons as to why you pray. You pray because life is chaotic and you want peace. You pray because you have specific needs that you want to be fufilled. You pray because you are anxious and nervous about the future. You pray because you need God's guidance in your life.

Or perhaps you're not much into prayer these days. Maybe you've been burned by prayer in the past. You asked God to heal a friend, but the friend didn't get well. You asked God to restore a relationship, but you seem more distant now than ever before. You were faithful in spending time with God every day, but you still felt spiritually dry. So you gave up.

There are a lot of reasons we pray . . . and there are a lot of reasons we don't pray. But if we're honest, we probably spend most of our prayer time in petition before God, asking him for specific things or outcomes. Now, there is nothing wrong with making requests to God. Jesus told his followers, "Whatever you ask for in prayer, believe that you have received it, and it will be yours" (Mark 11:24). We are right to ask for God's help whenever we need it.

But our *motive* is key. Are we asking God for what we want, or are we trusting him for what he wants for us? If prayer is just about asking for what we want, we will get burned out on it pretty quickly. Prayer is about much more than that! It's about building a relationship with God. It's about learning to hear his voice. It's about creating a habit of casting our worries and cares on him so that we can carry a lighter load. When prayer is simply transactional, we miss out on its richness. We miss out on a real relationship with God.

Consider Mother Teresa's approach to prayer. In an interview with CBS news anchor Dan Rather, she was asked what she said to God when she prayed. "I don't say anything," she replied. "I listen." Dan Rather then asked, "Well, okay . . . when God speaks to you, what does he say?" Mother Teresa replied, "He doesn't say anything. He listens."[6]

READ | MATTHEW 6:6–13

REFLECT

1. Jesus prayed this prayer (called the "Lord's Prayer") in the Sermon on the Mount—a series of teachings he did in the region of Galilee. Before he prayed, he warned the crowd against praying like the hypocrites: "For they love to pray standing in the synagogues and on the corners of the streets, that they may be seen by men" (verse 5 NKJV). How did Jesus begin this prayer? What did he ask for? How did he end the prayer?

2. Jesus was God's Son. He was intimate with the Father. He knew his Father's heart and his ways. Still, he prayed. *Why* do you think Jesus prayed?

3. What are your prayers usually like? What is your motive behind what you pray for? If you're not in a praying season right now, why is that?

4. How do you want your prayer life to change? Explain your response.

PRAY | Model your prayer today after the Lord's Prayer. Praise God, petition God, ask for forgiveness, and then end your prayer in praise and for God's will to be done on earth.

Day 4

MEETING GOD AT ROCK BOTTOM

God met Jacob when he was at rock bottom. He had deceived his father and brother, trying to take something that wasn't his to take. He had been forced to flee from his home. He was now alone in the wilderness. But God, instead of chastising Jacob or turning away from him, met him right where he was—at Bethel—and made a promise to be with him.

You probably know what rock bottom feels like. You remember hitting it after losing a job, a spouse, or a friend. You recall feeling its grip in a time of loneliness, sadness, or anxiety that just wouldn't go away. Rock bottom looks different for everyone, but everyone's rock bottom is humbling. But it is there, when we've been stripped away from everything that once made us feel good about ourselves, that we are primed to hear God's voice.

Perhaps this is why Jacob could hear God so clearly when he hit his rock bottom. He had been stripped of everything and everyone he loved. He was alone and uncertain of the future. It was at this point that he could clearly hear the voice of God.

No matter how rocky our rock bottom is, and no matter how many times we've been there, God speaks to us in the pit. And he doesn't just speak to us. He invites us into his work. He promises to be near us. We may experience the consequences of whatever actions brought us to where we are, but God isn't going to punish us for being there. He always has a plan to get us out of that pit we've created for ourselves and to use us for his purposes.

READ | ACTS 9:1–20

REFLECT

1. Saul, later known as Paul, was a self-proclaimed Hebrew of Hebrews (see Philippians 3:4–6). He was from the elite tribe of Benjamin and studied as a Pharisee. He would eventually become the most prominent voice in the New Testament and dedicate his life to proclaiming the gospel—but that's not the case when we first encounter him. What happened to him at Damascus? How do you think he was feeling during the three days that he couldn't see, eat, or drink?

2. Why do you think Jesus chose to meet Paul, the great persecutor of Christians, in the way that he did? According to verse 18, what impact did this rock-bottom moment have on Paul? How does Paul's reaction to his rock-bottom moment differ from Jacob's?

3. When is the last time you hit rock bottom? How did you experience God in that place?

4. Considering how God treated those in Scripture during their worst moments, how do you think God feels about you in your worst moments? What does Paul's story tell you about who God uses for the furthering of his kingdom?

PRAY | End your time in prayer. Thank God for seasons on the mountaintop and at rock bottom. He is at work in both. Ask him to be present in your life today in surprising ways, even if you feel unequipped or you feel you are in the pit. Ask him to make himself known to you.

Day 5

CATCH UP & READ AHEAD

Use this time to go back and complete any of the study and reflection questions from previous days this week that you weren't able to finish. Make a note below of any revelations you've had and reflect on any growth or personal insights you've gained.

Spend the next two days reading chapters 6–7 of *God Never Gives Up on You*. Use the space below to make note of anything in the chapters that stands out to you or encourages you.

Schedule

WEEK 3

BEFORE GROUP MEETING	Read chapters 6–7 of *God Never Gives Up on You* Read the Welcome section (page 47)
GROUP MEETING	Discuss the Connect questions Watch the video teaching for session 3 Discuss the questions that follow as a group Do the closing exercise and pray (pages 47–54)
PERSONAL STUDY - DAY 1	Complete the daily study (pages 57–58)
PERSONAL STUDY - DAY 2	Complete the daily study (pages 59–60)
PERSONAL STUDY - DAY 3	Complete the daily study (pages 61–62)
PERSONAL STUDY - DAY 4	Complete the daily study (pages 63–64)
CATCH UP & READ AHEAD - DAY 5 (before week 4 group meeting)	Read chapters 8–9 of *God Never Gives Up on You* Complete any unfinished personal studies

LIVING WITH A LOUSE

For in the day of trouble he will keep me safe in his dwelling; he will hide me in the shelter of his sacred tent and set me high upon a rock.

PSALM 27:5

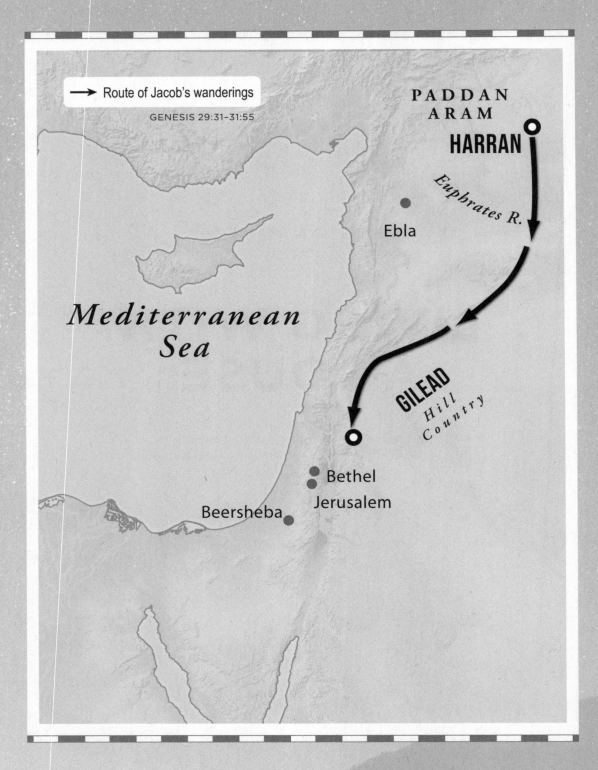

Route of Jacob's wanderings

GENESIS 29:31–31:55

PADDAN
ARAM

HARRAN

Euphrates R.

Ebla

*Mediterranean
Sea*

GILEAD
*Hill
Country*

Bethel

Jerusalem

Beersheba

Welcome |

Our greatest call as followers of Jesus, second to loving God, is to love one another (see Mark 12:29–31). The perfect embodiment of this calling is a beautiful picture: the church of God loving one another, celebrating one another, and sharing with one another. A scene where everyone gets along, with pictures of happy, joyful, smiling faces everywhere.

If only this were the reality! An honest look at life in our world today paints a much different picture. Sure, there are moments where we all get along. But inevitably, *that* person shows up to disrupt the tranquility. You know *that* person. The one who gets on your nerves. The one you don't trust. The one who is in your community whether you like it or not—and you don't like it. The one who makes it difficult to follow God's command to love one another. The *louse* in your life.

In the animal world, a louse is an insect that lives on the skin. In the human world, a louse is a person who gets under your skin. It's hard to know what to do with a louse. How do you get rid of him or her? And why did God allow that person to come into your life in the first place?

You will explore these questions this week as you learn about the louse in Jacob's life, Laban, and how he responded to him. For the first time, you will learn something from Jacob's example that you *should* model. For Jacob proved to be strategic in his interactions with Laban, trusting in God and making decisions motivated by faith rather than fear.

Connect | 15 MINUTES

Get the session started by choosing one of these questions to discuss as a group:

- What is a key insight or takeaway from last week's personal study that you would like to share with the group?

    — *or* —

- Without naming names, think about a past "louse" in your life—someone who got under your skin. Why do you think that person affected you in that way?

Watch | 20 MINUTES

Now watch the video for this session. Below is an outline of the key points covered during the teaching. Record any thoughts or concepts that stand out to you.

I. The word *home* means different things to different people.

    A. From some, the word *home* brings up images of an environment that is comfortable, safe, and cozy. But for others, it could be that the mental picture is not as positive.

    B. Jacob ultimately had to work another seven years for Laban to marry Rachel. The fact he was now married to two sisters created all kinds of tensions, strife, and rivalries in the family.

    C. For Jacob, home was not a place of peace but one of continual crisis. All the while, he had to live with a louse—his uncle Laban.

II. The arrival of children in Jacob's family only serves to increase the tension.

    A. Leah bore four sons to Jacob in a row. Each of the son's names documented the hurt that she felt.

        1. *Reuben* means "look, a son," and sounds like the Hebrew for "he has seen my misery," a sign that God had seen Leah in her affliction.

2. *Simeon* means "the Lord heard," a thinly veiled barb at Rachel.

3. *Levi* means "connect," a lament from Leah of her lack of connection to Jacob.

4. *Judah* means "praise God." In the end, Leah recognized she could be thankful to God.

B. Rachel was so envious that she gave her maid, Bilhah, to Jacob so she could build a family through her (see Genesis 30:3). Bilhah bore two sons.

1. *Dan* means "vindication," a sign of how Rachel was feeling.

2. *Naphtali* means "struggle," indicating that Rachel was in an all-out fight with Leah.

C. Leah then arranged for her maid, Zilpah, to step into the fray. Zilpah bore two sons.

1. *Gad* means "lucky," another possible barb at Rachel.

2. *Asher* means "happy," though we have to assume Rachel didn't feel Leah was "lucky" or congratulate her in her "happiness."

D. The turmoil around the dinner table in Jacob's household must have been insane. Rachel and Leah despised each other. It was a battle of wills and wombs.

III. Jacob is present in body in the family but absent in mind.

A. If only Jacob had demonstrated some leadership in his life. If only he had stood up to Laban. If only he had taken up Leah's cause. If only he had said no to sleeping with women who were not his wives.

B. The scandal of Jacob's family is disturbing. But if we're honest, it is also assuring. The Bible makes it clear that God can used flawed people like Jacob.

C. God can flick everything into healing mode. No family is beyond the possibility of a miracle. God did this in Jacob's case by allowing Rachel to become pregnant (see Genesis 30:23).

IV. Jacob finally takes a stand against Laban.

    A. Laban changed Jacob's wages ten times in six years to make sure the younger man stayed empty-handed. Finally, Jacob confronted Laban and told him the jig was up.

    B. Jacob asked for every speckled and spotted sheep, lamb, and goat from Laban's flock to be his wages (see Genesis 30:32–33). Laban agreed—and then promptly cheated Jacob again.

    C. Jacob didn't react in anger. Instead, he set about the task of building his flock (see Genesis 30:37–39). Jacob grew richer and acquired huge flocks and servants, camels, and donkeys.

V. We often ask where God is in the midst of our chaos.

    A. Jacob was left with two options in his dealings with Laban. He could trust God or grow anxious. For what seems like the first time, Jacob made the right choice and headed back home.

    B. Jacob's story teaches us that we can't fight the "Labans" in our lives on their terms. Instead, we need to respond to the Labans in our lives with faith in God.

    C. God puts Labans into our lives not to torment us but to teach us. God uses peculiar people to bring out the best in his people.

Discuss | 35 MINUTES

Discuss what you just watched by answering the following questions. There are some suggested questions below to help you begin your discussion, but feel free to pick any of the additional questions as time allows.

Suggested Questions

1. Consider the dynamics that were at play in Jacob's household—all the tensions, rivalries, and struggles between Leah and Rachel that would have significantly impacted the family. In your experience, how do tensions like this affect life at home? What do you imagine daily life was like for Jacob, Leah, Rachel, and their children?

2. Consider the meaning behind the names that Leah and Rachel gave to all the sons born of Jacob. What do these names tell you about how each woman was feeling?

3. Read Genesis 30:31–34. How did Laban deceive Jacob yet again? When is a time in your life that you were deceived or manipulated by someone close to you?

4. Jacob employed an unusual strategy to increase his flocks (see Genesis 30:37–43). While there is no evidence this strategy had anything to do with the sheep or goats producing spotted and speckled offspring, it does reveal that Jacob was operating to Laban's deception with faith rather than fear. When is a time you responded to your Laban, your "louse," with this kind of faith? What was the result of your actions?

Additional Questions

5. Jacob appears to be silent in the midst of the quarrel between Rachel and Leah. The Bible does not relate any examples of him trying to step in to resolve the difficulties. Instead, he compounds the tensions by agreeing to have children with Bilhah and Zilpah. Based on what you know of Jacob, why do you think he took this course?

6. Read Genesis 30:22–24. Rachel, who up to this point had been unable to conceive, finally gave birth to a son. How did she respond when she discovered she was able to give birth? What faith did she place in God by naming her son *Joseph*, "may he add"?

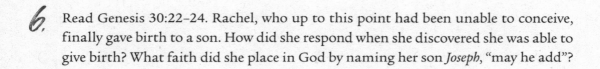

7. God appeared to Jacob in a dream and said, "I have seen all that Laban has been doing to you" (Genesis 31:12). In spite of Jacob's flaws and missteps, the Lord had not given up on him. How do you think Jacob felt when he received this message from God? How do you think this dream encouraged him to take action and return home?

8. We all have Labans in our lives—those people who actively try to deceive us, manipulate us, monopolize us, and drag us down. Why do you think God allows these kind of "louses" in our lives? What have you learned from a louse, either past or present?

Respond | 10 MINUTES

Pick one of the characters from today's study—Jacob, Leah, Rachel, Laban, or even Bilhah or Zilpah—with whom you identify the most. Use the space below to reflect on why you identify with this character at this point in the story. Share what you wrote with the group.

Pray | 10 MINUTES

End your time by praying together. Ask God to help you deal with the louses in your life in a loving way. Ask if anyone has any prayer requests to share. Write those requests down in the space below so you and your group members can pray about them in the week ahead.

Name	Request

PERSONAL STUDY

Home is meant to be a safe haven—a place of comfort and rest—but we know this isn't always the case. Sometimes, home is the last place you want to be. But even when this is true, you always have a safe haven in Christ. As you explore this theme in this week's personal study, write down your responses to the questions in the spaces provided, as you will be given a few minutes to share your insights at the start of the next session if you are doing this study with others. If you are reading *God Never Gives Up on You* while doing this study, read chapters 6–7.

Day 1

FEELINGS OF INADEQUACY

Family life for Jacob during his time in Paddan Aram was filled with strife, tension, and dysfunction. Leah competed for his attention and affection. Rachel competed with Leah for children. Some of the children's names reflected the conflict. What a legacy to inherit!

It's tempting to read Rachel and Leah's story and judge them. Why couldn't they work together and live together? But we have to remember that they were pitted against each other by their father from the start. It was *Laban* who tricked Jacob into marrying Leah instead of Rachel. Of course, Jacob was disappointed. But Leah felt the misery as well: "It is because the LORD has seen my misery. Surely my husband will love me now. . . . Because the LORD heard that I am not loved, he gave me this one too. . . . Now at last my husband will become attached to me, because I have borne him three sons" (Genesis 29:32–34).

Rachel, for her part, told Jacob, "Give me children, or I'll die!" (Genesis 30:1). Each woman felt she wasn't enough for Jacob—one because she wasn't the chosen wife, the other because she wasn't able to conceive. At the root of their struggle is one we all know well: a feeling of inadequacy. Both women thought if they could just get Jacob's attention, have his affection, and have his children, they would feel like they were enough. But, of course, neither woman could ultimately be fulfilled by Jacob's attention, affection, or approval.

Leah perhaps realized this truth with the birth of her fourth son, Judah, saying, "This time I will praise the LORD" (Genesis 29:35). Competition, jealousy, and inadequacy can all be driven out by love. When we know and trust that we are fully loved for who we are, not for who we want to be, our focus shifts. It is no longer on the other person and how he or she reacts or doesn't react. It is on the God who loves us and the Savior who set us free.

READ | PSALM 139:1–5, 13–17

REFLECT

1. In this psalm, David reflects on the omnipresence and omniscience of God—the ability for God to be everywhere and know everything. This means that God knows everything we do and say, when we sit and when we rise, all of our thoughts. Imagine Rachel and Leah reading this psalm. Which parts of it would they most need to hear? How would this psalm have encouraged them in their feelings of inadequacy?

2. David states that each of us is "fearfully and wonderfully made" (verse 14). How does he describe God's works? What does this mean about who you are in God's eyes?

3. Where do you feel inadequate in your life? How do you feel about this inadequacy? What behaviors do you think are motivated by these feelings?

4. Based on what you read in this psalm, what value does God place on you? How could this psalm reframe your thoughts when you are feeling that you are not enough?

PRAY | Meditate on today's psalm as your prayer time. Read it out loud or to yourself. Let the words wash over you. Notice which verses stick out to you and why.

Day 2

IN A HOUSE
WITH A LOUSE

Jacob lived under Laban's roof for twenty years. Two decades. That is a long time to be dealing with the same louse, much less living in the same house as the louse. You can imagine the tension, arguments, and frustration that arose.

We have all had to deal with louses, and many of us have had to live with one. Perhaps, like Jacob, yours is an in-law—a person you are supposed to respect, but it is difficult to respect them because they just get under your skin. But this is the thing with louses—they get to us. They get in our heads. They consume our thoughts. We think of witty retorts we will give them the next time they give us a hard time. We think about the ways we can get revenge. The ways we are better than they are. We focus on the louse, which only exacerbates the problem.

Jacob eventually triumphed over Laban not because he figured out a clever way to get back at him or get revenge on him but because he finally took his focus off of Laban. He could have gotten angry and resentful at Laban's deceit. He could have lamented the fact that he had been duped yet again and given up. But what did he do instead? He focused on growing his flock and doing what he needed to do to get back home. He didn't sabotage Laban's flock. He didn't argue with Laban or fight. He simply put his head down and got to work.

When we take our focus off our louse and focus on what is needed to do God's work, our louse will lose his or her power over us. Then, and only then, can we place that power back in God's hands, who, unlike our louse, is for us, with us, and ready to help us in our time of need.

READ | Isaiah 26:1–6

REFLECT

1. Isaiah prophesied to Israel about how they would suffer under conquering nations. He also prophesied about the time when God would restore the people of Israel as a nation. This passage of Scripture, known as "The Song of Judah," portrays a people who trust fully in God even when the nations threaten them. They know he is their rock and salvation. According to verse 3, who does God keep in perfect peace, and why?

2. What did God do to Israel's enemies (see verses 5–6)?

3. Think about a current louse in your life. How often do you think about that person? What are your thoughts like toward that individual?

4. What would it look like for you to take the focus off your louse and put it on God? What do you think the Lord is trying to teach you through this trying relationship?

PRAY | End your time in prayer. Instead of asking God to fix your louse or get rid of that person from your life, ask what he is trying to teach you. Ask him to help you keep your thoughts stayed on him when your mind wanders to this person. Ask him to remind you that he is your everlasting rock and that when you stand on him, nothing and no one can shake you.

Day 3

GOD ALWAYS SEES US

At the beginning of this week's message, you were asked to close your eyes and think about the word *home*. What came to mind in that moment? What feelings arose? What images came up for you?

While home brings happy memories for some, it brings more complicated memories to others. Perhaps you grew up in a home full of tension and strife, just like we saw in the story of Rachel and Leah. Perhaps your louse was always present, looming over you. Perhaps there was fighting, abuse, and a general feeling of not being safe. Perhaps the home you are in now feels this way.

While home is meant to bring shelter and warmth—while it is meant to be the place that protects us—this is sadly not always the case. If it wasn't for you, you may have wondered, *Where is God in this situation? Does he care? Does he see me? Does he know?*

Jacob probably wondered this at times. As he found himself desperately wanting to flee a home that had grown toxic, he likely remembered God's promise at Bethel to be with him and wondered if that promise still held for him. If it did, then why was God sitting idly by while Laban deceived him time and again and his family was at each other's throats?

Jacob received his answer in the form of a vision that you will read in today's study. It was a reminder that God had not left him and had remembered the promise he made at Bethel. God cares for you in this way too, whether you are dealing with memories of a difficult home in your past or wrestling with a difficult home life now. God sent us the ultimate Savior in Jesus, and Jesus left us with the ultimate comforter in his Spirit.

READ | GENESIS 31:11–13 AND JOHN 14:15–20

REFLECT

1. How does God assure Jacob of his plans for his life in the passage from Genesis? Of what does he remind Jacob? What does he tell him to do?

2. How does Jesus describe the Holy Spirit in the passage from John? What promise does Jesus make to his followers in verse 18?

3. Think about your home life growing up and your home life now. When have you felt unsafe, unseen, or uncared for?

4. How can the presence of the Holy Spirit comfort you, whether you are dealing with difficult memories from the past or a difficult home life today?

PRAY | Ask God for what you need. Do you need healing from trauma or memories from the past that you've tried to forget? Do you need healing in your home today? Ask the Holy Spirit to intervene and be your advocate. Believe that healing is possible.

Day 4
READY FOR A RETURN

Jacob had spent twenty years in Paddan Aram by the time Joseph, the first child with his wife Rachel, finally came on the scene. Immediately after, Jacob approaches Laban and says, "Send me on my way so I can go back to my own homeland" (Genesis 30:25). Jacob had fled his homeland to escape his brother, but now he was determined to return there once again. Some historical context can help us understand the sudden urgency on his part.

In the ancient world, a woman who could not have children did not have an established place with her husband. She could be ostracized by her family and community or sent to live with relatives. So it was that when Rachel finally gave birth to Joseph, her place with her huband was no longer tenuous. Jacob finally felt free to leave with her.[7]

But Jacob was still facing an enemy back home. As we read, "Esau held a grudge against Jacob because of the blessing his father had given him. He said to himself, 'The days of mourning for my father are near; then I will kill my brother Jacob'" (Genesis 27:41). While Jacob's plan was always to go back (see 28:20–22), he likely felt hesitant to return.

Perhaps you, like Jacob, know what it's like to run away, and you know what it's like to be called by God to go home. Maybe you literally ran away from your hometown, but now you're feeling a nudge to return. Or maybe you left the church and are considering visiting again. Or maybe you've avoided your family for years but are feeling called to pick up the phone. Or maybe you abandoned a relationship but are feeling called to reconcile.

As scary as it sounds, if you are feeling called to return home—or to a relationship or community that you have run from in the past—you can trust God's timing. Your heart is ready for a return. And your heavenly Father will be with you every step of the way.

READ | EXODUS 3:1–12

REFLECT

1. Moses had a complicated relationship with his past. Born a Hebrew, he was raised by Pharaoh's daughter. When he was older, he killed an Egyptian who was beating a Hebrew slave. Worried he would get caught, he fled to a place called Midian. Just when he thought he had left Egypt for good, the Lord called him to face Pharaoh (and his past) and lead the Israelites to freedom. How does Moses react to God's call?

2. Considering Moses' complicated history with his past, how do you think he was feeling about God's plan? What assurance does the Lord give to Moses?

3. Think about a time you returned "home" after being away, whether that was a literal home or something else. What was that homecoming like? How did it bring healing?

4. What relationship or circumstance from your past is still unresolved and in need of God's healing? Could the Lord be calling you to go "home" and face your past? If so, how do you feel about this calling?

PRAY | End your time in prayer. If it feels right, remove your shoes as Moses did to remind yourself that you are in God's presence, which is holy. Ask God what he is calling you to do today. Talk to him about the open wounds in your life that still need healing.

Day 5

CATCH UP & READ AHEAD

Use this time to go back and complete any of the study and reflection questions from previous days this week that you weren't able to finish. Make a note below of any revelations you've had and reflect on any growth or personal insights you've gained.

Spend the next two days reading chapters 8–9 in *God Never Gives Up on You*. Use the space below to make note of anything in the chapters that stands out to you or encourages you.

Schedule

WEEK 4

BEFORE GROUP MEETING	Read chapters 8–9 of *God Never Gives Up on You* Read the Welcome section (page 69)
GROUP MEETING	Discuss the Connect questions Watch the video teaching for session 4 Discuss the questions that follow as a group Do the closing exercise and pray (pages 69–76)
PERSONAL STUDY – DAY 1	Complete the daily study (pages 79–80)
PERSONAL STUDY – DAY 2	Complete the daily study (pages 81–82)
PERSONAL STUDY – DAY 3	Complete the daily study (pages 83–84)
PERSONAL STUDY – DAY 4	Complete the daily study (pages 85–86)
CATCH UP & READ AHEAD - DAY 5 (before week 5 group meeting)	Read chapters 10–12 of *God Never Gives Up on You* Complete any unfinished personal studies

SESSION FOUR

WRESTLING WITH GOD

You were taught, with regard to your former way of life, to put off your old self, which is being corrupted by its deceitful desires; to be made new in the attitude of your minds; and to put on the new self, created to be like God in true righteousness and holiness.

EPHESIANS 4:22-24

Route of Jacob's wanderings

GENESIS 32:1–33:20

Mediterranean Sea

Laish
(Dan)

Hazor

Sea of
Galilee

GILEAD
Hill Country

Dothan

Jordan R.

Succoth
Penuel

Shechem

Jabbok R.

MAHANAIM

Aphek

Bethel

Gezer

Salem

Timnah

Ephrath
(Bethlehem)

Adullam

Kiriath Arba
(Hebron)

Mamre

Dead
Sea

Arnon R.

Beersheba

Negev

Zered R.

Beer Lahai Roi?

EDOM

Land
of
Seir

Desert   of   Paran

Welcome |

All humans have what is known as a fight-or-flight response. When we encounter stressful situations, our bodies release chemicals that compel us to either face the danger (fight) or move away from it (flight). The fight-or-flight response is essential in keeping us aware of threats and prepared—in one way or the other—to deal with them. But what's interesting is that the response kicks in whether the threat is real or just imagined.

In Jacob's story, we see that his fight-or-flight response kicked in when he stole Esau's blessing and then learned that his older brother wanted to kill him. Jacob opted for flight in this situation, journeying some 400 miles from Beersheba to Harran to escape the wrath of his older brother. Jacob ran away from his past—and from his mistakes—and managed to stay on the run for twenty years. But eventually, he knew that he had to return home and come face-to-face with Esau. It was time for him to stop taking *flight* and instead *fight*.

As you will see in this session, it was actually God who made this apparent to Jacob. In one of the most mysterious scenes in the Bible, the Lord appeared to Jacob along the banks of the Jabbok River and wrestled with him throughout the night. It was a bout that would forever change his life. From that point forward, he would no longer be known as Jacob but as Israel, for he had "struggled with God . . . and have overcome" (Genesis 32:28).

Connect | 15 MINUTES

Get the session started by choosing one of these questions to discuss as a group:

- What is a key insight or takeaway from last week's personal study that you would like to share with the group?

  — *or* —

- Think about a time you ran away from your past. What did running away look like? Did you literally run away to a place or do something else?

Watch | 20 MINUTES

Now watch the video for this session. Below is an outline of the key points covered during the teaching. Record any thoughts or concepts that stand out to you.

I. Jacob's dark night of the soul.

    A. Jacob's journey had started out well. So bright and full of hope. But his deception of Esau had led to him fleeing his homeland and traveling to Harran—and his dark night began.

    B. Harran was the land of Laban. It was the place where Jacob spent twenty long years getting acquainted with the taste of his own medicine. But now, it was time to go back home.

    C. But there was a problem. In fact, the *same* problem that had forced Jacob to flee in the first place. Jacob was leaving the house of a louse to face a brute of a brother.

II. Jacob prepares to meet Esau.

    A. Jacob sent a message to Esau to let him know he was back in town. His servants returned with the message that Esau was coming to meet him with 400 men (see Genesis 32:6).

B. Jacob divided his household, livestock, and possessions into two camps (see Genesis 32:7–8). It was perhaps the darkest night of the soul that Jacob had yet faced.

C. Jacob prayed, "Please deliver me from the hand of my brother, from the hand of Esau, for I fear him" (Genesis 32:11 ESV). This was the prayer of a man who had learned his lesson.

III. Jacob wrestles with God by the banks of the Jabbok River.

A. The Jabbok River was the place where God would bring Jacob face-to-face with himself and set him on a new path. The text of what happens next is terse and gives us few details: "Jacob was left alone; and a Man wrestled with him until the breaking of day" (Genesis 32:24 NKJV).

B. At one point Jacob had the best of his opponent. But the man settled the matter once and for all with a deft jab to Jacob's hip that left him writhing like a gored matador.

C. The jab cleared Jacob's vision, and he realized that he was tangling with God. He grabbed hold of the man and cried, "I will not let You go unless You bless me!" (Genesis 32:26 NKJV).

IV. Jacob receives a new name from God.

A. Jacob was asking God, "Do I matter to you?" Given a face-to-face encounter with the Almighty, we would ask the same. "God, do you know who I am?"

B. We find God's response in Jacob's story. The Lord asks him to give his name. In that moment, Jacob is admitting that he is a heel-holder, cheater, hustler, smart operator, and a fraud.

C. God says, "From now on you will be called Israel, because you have fought with God and with men and have won" (Genesis 32:28 NLT). His new name would reflect his new strength.

D. Jacob sent his family out first, dividing the children among their mothers. First went Bilhah and Zilpah. Next was Leah, the wife he didn't want. Finally came Rachel, the wife he loved, and their son, Joseph. The meaning was lost on no one. It was a "Jacob" decision.

V. Jacob reunites with his brother.

A. Jacob limps his way across the Jordan River. "He crossed over before [Esau] and bowed himself to the ground seven times, until he came near to his brother" (Genesis 33:3 NKJV).

B. "Esau ran to meet him, and embraced him, and fell on his neck and kissed him, and they wept" (Genesis 33:4 NKJV). Esau wept because his brother was home. Israel wept because he had come face-to-face with his past—only to find that his past held no power over his life.

C. The message of the Esau event is that you can't move past your past without God's help. But God says you are no longer Jacob. You are now Israel, and he fights for you.

Discuss | 35 MINUTES

Discuss what you just watched by answering the following questions. There are some suggested questions below to help you begin your discussion, but feel free to pick any of the additional questions as time allows.

Suggested Questions

1. Jacob took a step of faith by returning to Beersheba and the last of his youth. On the way, he was met by angels, which was encouraging (see Genesis 32:1). But he was also met with reports that Esau was moving to meet him with 400 men. Read Jacob's prayer in Genesis 32:9–12. What does this tell you about how he was feeling about his reunion with his brother, Esau? When have you prayed a desperate prayer like this?

2. Jacob's encounter with "the man" at the Jabbok River warrants a place in the great hall of holy moments. Moses on Mount Sinai. Elijah on Mount Carmel. Jesus in the Jordan River. What strikes you the most about this story and its mysterious character? What question was Jacob *really* asking when he asked for a blessing?

3. "Then the man said, 'Your name will no longer be Jacob, but Israel, because you have struggled with God and with humans and have overcome" (Genesis 32:28). What does the name *Israel* mean? Why is it significant considering Jacob's story and history? When has God helped you wrestle with your past in a productive way?

4. Read Genesis 33:1–15. Why do you think Esau was able to forgive Jacob and embrace him? When have you experienced this kind of undeserved forgiveness from someone in your life with whom you've been in conflict?

Additional Questions

5. Jacob went to great lengths to protect himself and his family from Esau and his 400 men (see Genesis 32:7–16; 33:1–3). What are some ways in the past that you have protected yourself and others from harm when you anticipated a conflict was coming?

6. Why do you think the man Jacob wrestled asked Jacob what his name was? If God were to ask you that today in light of your past, what would you say?

7. When Jacob saw Esau, he went out ahead of his family and "bowed down to the ground seven times as he approached his brother" (Genesis 33:3). Esau ran to Jacob, embraced him, and wept. What do you think this moment was like for Jacob and Esau? When have you experienced this kind of a reunion in your life?

8. Jacob physically wrestled with God until daybreak. What is something you need to "wrestle" with God about—something from your past, a sin, or a mistake that you haven't worked through? Are you open to working through these issues with him? Why or why not?

Respond | 10 MINUTES

God gave Jacob a new name after he wrestled with him. Think about a defining moment you have had with God—your own "wrestling match." What new name would you give yourself after this moment to mark how you changed? Write down that name and what it means to you.

Pray | 10 MINUTES

End your time by praying together as a group. Thank God for making you a new creation through Jesus. Ask if anyone has any prayer requests to share. Write those requests down in the space below so you and your group members can pray about them in the week ahead.

Name   Request

_____   _____

_____   _____

_____   _____

_____   _____

_____   _____

_____   _____

_____   _____

_____   _____

_____   _____

_____   _____

PERSONAL STUDY

We've all spent time on the "wrestling mat" of life—times of wrestling with ourselves, with our past, and even with God. Think about how this has looked in your own life as you dig deeper into the passages of Scripture that you will study this week. Write down your responses to the questions below in the spaces provided, as you will be given a few minutes to share your insights at the start of the next session if you are doing this study with others. If you are reading *God Never Gives Up on You* while doing this study, read chapters 8–9.

DARK NIGHT OF THE SOUL

John of the Cross was a Catholic priest and mystic who coined the phrase the "Dark Night of the Soul" as the title of a poem that he wrote in the sixteenth century.[8] Ever since, people of faith have resonated with those words. The darkness of the soul is its own type of darkness . . . a difficult period of time where you feel far from God. It's lonely, desperate, and desolate.

Jacob experienced more than one dark night of the soul, and you probably have as well. Nights when you doubt God's plan or even his existence. Nights when you are haunted by your past, unable to escape it. Nights when you are searching the night sky, wondering when and if dawn will ever break. But dark nights of the soul are just that— a *night*. They don't last forever. Yes, they will likely last more than one literal night. But they are seasons, and seasons always come to an end. As Eugene Peterson wrote, "The accounts of saints who tell of the 'dark nights' of the soul are familiar. Their search for God seems endless and futile, but is broken into by moments of ecstasy when they find (or are found by) the one they sought."[9]

Jacob's dark night that we discussed in this session was the one leading up to him meeting Esau again for the first time in twenty years. When Jacob left Esau, he was running for his life. He had stolen Esau's birthright—what was most precious to a firstborn son at the time—and his brother was out for revenge. We can assume Jacob's dark night of the soul was riddled with fear, anxiety, and shame. Yet he was found by the one he sought: God.

God will meet us in our dark nights of the soul. In our shame, fear, and anxiety, he is there. The darkness clouds our vision, but rest assured, the One we seek we will find.

READ | GENESIS 32:22–24 AND PSALM 30:1–5

REFLECT

1. How do you think Jacob felt as he watched his family cross the river without him? The passage says that Jacob was "left alone, and a man wrestled with him" (Genesis 32:24). What is significant about Jacob's being *alone* before he wrestled God?

2. David is believed to have penned Psalm 30, but it could have been written by Jacob. How does this psalm parallel Jacob's experience?

3. When was your darkest night of the soul? What led you there? How did you experience God during that time?

4. What feels dark in your life today? How could Jacob's story or David's words in Psalm 30 give you hope in the midst of that darkness?

PRAY | If you are in a dark night of the soul, know that you are not alone. Many other saints have gone before you. So ask God to meet you during this time. Seek him and you will find him. Pray as Jacob did in Genesis 32:11, filling in your own requests: "Save me, I pray, from _____, for I am afraid _____."

Day 2
WRESTLING WITH YOURSELF

In Psalm 30, which you read yesterday, David praised God for not letting him be overcome by his enemies. But when it comes to facing our past, we are often our *own* worst enemy. Just think about Jacob leading up to his encounter with Esau. Jacob was terrified. He sent Esau gifts. He divided up his camp in case they were attacked by Esau's men. He prepared for him and those he loved to die. And for what? All to discover that Esau had forgiven him and was looking forward to seeing him again, not killing him.

We tend to do this with our past. We magnify events in our minds until we are consumed by fear and guilt and anxiety. We assume the worst outcome. We think our friend or family member is still angry with us and resents us. We freeze our past in time, as if no one and nothing has changed. We still feel guilt about what happened back then.

But what if, as in this situation between Jacob and Esau, that old conflict has been resolved in the other person's mind and heart? What if the person you hurt has forgiven you? What if the shame you feel is self-imposed? What if you are your own worst enemy?

We won't know this until we face our past, and as discussed during the group time, we can face our past only with God's help, whether that means wrestling with our own heart or returning to that person or place that brought us shame. People move on. They change. Releasing a difficult memory from our past might be what we need to release ourselves from it.

READ | GENESIS 33:4–12 AND ROMANS 8:1–2

REFLECT

1. Esau wept when he saw Jacob. What else did Esau do in this passage that proved he had forgiven his brother? How did Jacob respond to Esau's forgiveness?

2. In Paul's letter to the church in Rome, he laid out the basics of Christian theology. According to these verses, why is there no condemnation for those who are in Christ Jesus? Why can this be such a hard truth for us to accept and believe?

3. What mistake from your past do you need to forgive yourself for doing? Who was involved in that situation, if anyone? How do you think he or she feels about it today?

4. How might God be calling you to wrestle with these kinds of moments from your past? Do you need to confront someone else who was involved, or confront yourself, or forgive yourself? How could you ask God to help you wrestle with this moment?

PRAY | Ask God to help you work through any moments you identified from your past that still haunt you. Be open to what the Lord says, even if it's simply to accept his forgiveness.

Day 3

BLESS ME!

Jacob made an interesting demand of the man he was wrestling: "I will not let you go unless you bless me" (Genesis 32:26). This raises an interesting question. If you were wrestling with a stranger, what would you ask of that person? Maybe for the individual to have mercy on you, to let you go, to leave you alone?

Jacob had the opposite reaction. He clung to the stranger and demanded a blessing. This tells us that Jacob likely knew that he was wrestling with the divine. He had God's full attention, and he was going to take full advantage of it.

What would you ask God if you encountered him in the flesh? What would you want to know? As discussed in this week's teaching, when Jacob asked the stranger to "bless" him, he was really asking a much deeper question. He was asking if he *mattered* to God—whether, after all he had done and all that had happened—God still cared for him, as he said to him at Bethel, or if he had fallen from grace a few too many times.

When have you wondered this about yourself? Where have you turned for the answer? It's natural for us to look to external sources for validation. We want to know how our parents feel about us, or what our spouse thinks of us, or what our Instagram followers think of us. We think that if enough people tell us we are worthy, we will *feel* we are worthy. And when we receive this external validation, we feel good about ourselves for a while.

But what about when this *doesn't* happen—when our parents, our spouse, our followers don't give us the validation that we are needing? Then we don't feel good about ourselves. And if our worth and value depend on the fickle opinions of those around us, we will *never* have enough validation.

So the next time you catch yourself wondering if you matter, take a note from the flawed hero of our story. Don't ask everyone around you. Ask the only One who matters.

READ | GENESIS 32:25–29 AND EPHESIANS 1:11–14

REFLECT

1. Look at how Jacob asked the man for a blessing: "I will not let you go unless you bless me" (verse 26). How does this request for a blessing differ from the way Jacob received the blessing from his father, Isaac, which was meant for Esau (see Genesis 27)? What does this tell you about some of the ways in which Jacob had changed?

2. According to Paul in the passage from Ephesians, what does Christ reveal to us? When did Jesus make a plan for our lives—and what is that plan?

3. Where or to whom do you tend to look to validate who you are? How does this validation feel when you get it? How does it feel when you don't get this validation?

4. Read Ephesians 1:11–14 again. Is it easy for you to believe Paul's words in this passage? How has knowing Christ affected the way you answer the question, *Do I matter?*

PRAY | Ask God the same question Jacob did: *Do I matter?* Listen for what he has to say. Sit in this truth, even if it makes you uncomfortable: you matter because you matter to God.

Day 4

A NEW CREATION

Did you have a nickname as a kid? Maybe an affectionate one given to you by your parents? Maybe one given to you by teasing peers at school? Maybe a name you thought was awesome at the time but now you cringe at the memory of it? Sometimes the nicknames we went by as kids stick long into adulthood. Sometimes we get rid of them the first chance we get—once we move away from home and start introducing ourselves in a new way. We are no longer the same person we were then, and we want to mark this with our name.

This is what happens again and again in Scripture. The names of our forefathers and foremothers of the faith change after they go through a significant personal change. Sometimes it is God who changes their names, and sometimes it is the people themselves. Abram became Abraham. Sarai became Sarah. Saul became Paul. Jacob became Israel.

When the man blessed Jacob, he did so by changing his name: "Your name will no longer be Jacob, but Israel, because you have struggled with God and with humans and have overcome" (Genesis 32:28). The name *Israel* means "he struggles with God." Jacob had wrestled with God and wrestled with his past—the deceiving man who had been forced to flee his hometown twenty years before—and he had overcome.

What have you struggled with and overcome? How did you mark that moment in your life? Maybe, like Jacob, you started going by a new name. Or maybe you just felt like a new person, capable of doing more than you thought, grateful to have gotten through the difficult time, and grateful to no longer be the person you once were. Or maybe you still feel stuck in the past. If so, take comfort from the words of Paul that you will study today.

READ | 2 CORINTHIANS 5:14–17

REFLECT

1. As mentioned in a previous session, the apostle Paul knew what it meant to undergo a transformation. He, too, took on a new name after becoming a Christ follower, no longer going by Saul in Scripture but by Paul. Considering the apostle's past, what do you think he meant when he said, "The old has gone, the new is here" (verse 17)?

2. Paul writes, "So from now on we regard no one from a worldly point of view" (verse 16). What does it mean to regard another person from a *worldly* point of view? How is Paul saying that we should see each other (and ourselves) now that we are in Christ?

3. Do you believe in your heart that you can be transformed into a new creation—that you can change and be free from the mistakes of the past? Why or why not?

4. Are you hanging on to an old identity or "nickname" that no longer defines you? What would Jesus have to say about this old identity?

PRAY | Thank Jesus for making you a new creation. Ask him to help you believe that you have been transformed and made completely new in him. Remember that you are not *waiting* to be made new. As Paul said, the old is already gone and the new is *already here!*

Day 5

CATCH UP & READ AHEAD

Use this time to go back and complete any of the study and reflection questions from previous days this week that you weren't able to finish. Make a note below of any revelations you've had and reflect on any growth or personal insights you've gained.

Spend the next two days reading chapters 10–12 in *God Never Gives Up on You*. Use the space below to make note of anything in the chapters that stands out to you or encourages you.

Schedule

WEEK 5

BEFORE GROUP MEETING	Read chapters 10–12 of *God Never Gives Up on You* Read the Welcome section (page 91)
GROUP MEETING	Discuss the Connect questions Watch the video teaching for session 5 Discuss the questions that follow as a group Do the closing exercise and pray (pages 91–98)
PERSONAL STUDY – DAY 1	Complete the daily study (pages 101–102)
PERSONAL STUDY – DAY 2	Complete the daily study (pages 103–104)
PERSONAL STUDY – DAY 3	Complete the daily study (pages 105–106)
PERSONAL STUDY – DAY 4	Complete the daily study (pages 107–108)
WRAP IT UP	Connect with your group about the next study that you want to go through together

RETURNING HOME

I will instruct you and teach you in the way you should go;
I will counsel you with my loving eye on you.

PSALM 32:8

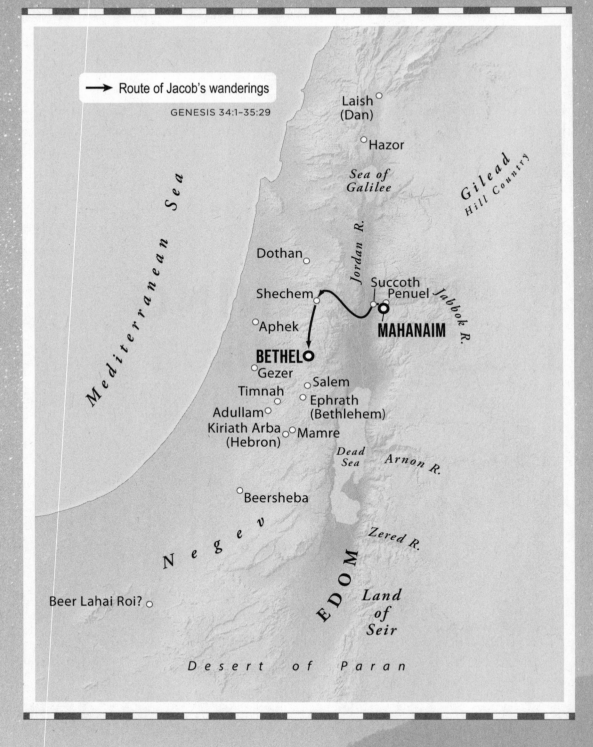

Route of Jacob's wanderings

GENESIS 34:1–35:29

Mediterranean Sea

Laish
(Dan)

Hazor

Sea of
Galilee

Gilead
Hill Country

Dothan

Jordan R.

Succoth
Penuel

Jabbok R.

Shechem

MAHANAIM

Aphek

BETHEL

Gezer

Salem

Timnah

Ephrath
(Bethlehem)

Adullam

Kiriath Arba
(Hebron)

Mamre

Dead
Sea

Arnon R.

Beersheba

N e g e v

Zered R.

EDOM

Land
of
Seir

Beer Lahai Roi?

D e s e r t   o f   P a r a n

Welcome |

It's tempting to see the Christian life as a straight road—a road in which we are always headed toward God. But if you've learned anything from this study, you know the Christian life is not linear, clean, neat, or predictable. It's filled with one wrong turn after another after another. While we learn from our mistakes, this does not keep us from making them in the future. Even the most faithful among us are prone to losing our way. It is our reality until the very end.

Now, it's one thing when we don't sense we have clear direction from God on which way to go or when there are multiple roads before us and grace to choose which one we will take. But sometimes, as we will see in this final session, God is explicit about the course that he wants us to take. In Jacob's case, he told the patriarch to "go back to the land where you were born" (Genesis 31:13 NCV). He was to go to Bethel. Instead, Jacob landed in the shadow of Shechem. It would prove to be a costly wrong move—perhaps the costliest of his life.

But the good news in Jacob's story—and in our stories—is that even when we take one wrong turn after another after another, we have a heavenly Father who is willing and able to step in and deliver us. Even when our actions land us in the shadow of Shechem, our God can guide us to freedom. He will lead us out of the mess that we have made, just as he led Jacob out of Shechem and back to Bethel. He never gave up on Jacob, and he will never give up on us.

Connect | 15 MINUTES

Get the session started by choosing one of these questions to discuss as a group:

- What is a key insight or takeaway from last week's personal study that you would like to share with the group?

  — *or* —

- Now that you're at the end of the study, how do you feel about Jacob? What new insights do you have about him?

Watch | 20 MINUTES

Now watch the video for this session. Below is an outline of the key points covered during the teaching. Record any thoughts or concepts that stand out to you.

I. The problem of disorientation.

    A. All of us get lost from time to time, even when the signs are clear in telling us where to go. This is especially true when we think we know better and choose our own route.

    B. Jacob had received clear signs from God about his destiny. But Jacob liked shortcuts, and his choices led him to a place he didn't expect. His disorientation continued when he reached Paddan Aram and had to work for twenty years to restore his spiritual bearings.

    C. A breakthrough occurred when Jacob wrestled with God at the Jabbok River. Jacob received a new name and clear instructions to go back to the land where he was born (see Genesis 31:13).

D. Jacob did not go back to Bethel but instead wandered over to Shechem. Once again, he lost his way. Once again, he and his family would suffer the consequences.

II. Jacob suffers the repercussions of settling for Shechem when the blessing is in Bethel.

A. Dinah, the seventh child of Leah (and Jacob's only daughter), was raped by the king of Shechem's son. We would expect Israel—"God fights"—to put up some kind of fight in the face of such injustice. But Jacob couldn't even muster the courage to file a complaint.

B. Dinah's brothers were not silent. They killed the men of Shechem, plundered the city, kidnapped the children, took the women, stole the flocks, and ransacked the shops.

C. Jacob did nothing to stop the plot. Instead, he placed his own safety above that of his daughter (see Genesis 34:30). In the end, he was just as guilty as Shechem.

D. We've all walked the road to Shechem. The shadow of Shechem is in our hearts. When we stop following God, the result is chaos. We break hearts, homes, covenants, and promises.

III. God speaks to Jacob instead of giving up on him for his failure.

A. We would think that God would abandon Jacob after this toxic season in Shechem. But instead, God comes to Jacob, and Jacob comes to his senses (see Genesis 35:1).

B. Jacob instructs his family to get rid of their idols. He buries them beneath a terebinth tree outside of Shechem (see Genesis 35:2–3). He reassumes the role as elder of the clan.

C. But Jacob is not the hero of his story. That title belongs to God and God alone. It was God who sought out Jacob, not Jacob who sought after God.

D. God even reaffirmed the promise he had made with Abraham. "The land which I gave Abraham and Isaac I give to you; and to your descendants after you I give this land" (Genesis 35:12 NKJV).

IV. What to make of our perpetually disoriented patriarch.

A. It is hard to know what to conclude about Jacob. But as we read his story, we can be amazed that God never benched him. The Lord never replaced Jacob with someone more polished and refined.

B. We don't know why God never gave up on Jacob. But we can all be grateful that he did not. For we all can identify with Jacob. We all have our own "limp."

C. God does not stand on a ladder and tell us to climb it and find him. Instead, he lowers a ladder down into the wilderness of our lives and finds us.

D. God does great things through the greatly broken. It's not the strength of the vessel that matters but the strength of the One who can use it.

Discuss | 35 MINUTES

Discuss what you just watched by answering the following questions. There are some suggested questions below to help you begin your discussion, but feel free to pick any of the additional questions as time allows.

Suggested Questions

1. God's instruction to Jacob when he left his uncle's home in Paddan Aram was to return to the land of his birth (see Genesis 31:3, 13). But instead, he went to the "city of Shechem in Canaan and camped within sight of the city" (33:18). When have you settled somewhere that you knew wasn't quite God's plan for you—whether that was a city, community, job, or church? Why did you settle there, and what happened as a result?

2. The story of Dinah's rape is difficult to read. Why do you think this story, and others like it, are included in Scripture? What does it tell us about the human condition?

3. When Jacob learned that his daughter had been raped, he "did nothing about it" until his sons came home (Genesis 34:5). When his sons arrived home and heard the news, they were "shocked and furious" (verse 7). Why do you think Jacob had such a different reaction from his sons? What was he more concerned about (see verse 30)?

4. Read Genesis 35:1–14. The time that Jacob and his family spent in Schechem had been a disaster on many levels. Yet God never gave up on Jacob or dismissed him because of his failings. Why do you think God continued to give Jacob second chances? How does this make you feel the wrong turns that you've taken at times?

Additional Questions

5. Dinah's words, thoughts, and feelings are not recorded in Scripture. Why do you think this is the case? What do you think she was thinking and feeling? If she had been given a voice in the matter, what do you think that she would have said?

6. God pursued Jacob . . . not the other way around. When have you felt that God was pursuing you even though you were walking away from him? What does your experience, and that of Jacob in the Bible, tell you about how God interacts with you?

7. What decision are you facing right now that could lead you either into the shadow of Shechem or the blessing of Bethel? How does today's study help to guide you?

8. The author of Hebrews tells us that "Jacob, when he was dying . . . worshiped as he leaned on the top of his staff" (Hebrews 11:21). Given everything that you have learned about Jacob and his character throughout this study, does this ending to his life surprise you? Who do you know who died faithfully in this way?

Respond | 10 MINUTES

Take a few minutes to write down three main takeaways that you will remember from this study, whether it's about our directionally challenged patriarch, about our persistent God, or about yourself. When everyone is finished writing, share your responses with the group.

Pray | 10 MINUTES

End your time by praying together. Thank God for giving you these last five weeks of studying his Word and learning more about him. Ask him to continue to teach you through Jacob's story. Ask if anyone has any prayer requests to share. Write those requests down in the space below so you and your group members can pray about them in the weeks ahead.

Name	Request

PERSONAL STUDY

We have all been guilty of settling for Shechem and pitching our tents on the outskirts of the city when God had the blessings of Bethel just waiting for us. If we are honest, it is difficult at times to wait on God and do the hard things that he is telling us to do. But the good news is God is patient with us. He is gracious. He never gives up on us. As you explore this theme in this week's personal study, write down your responses to the questions in the spaces provided. If you are reading *God Never Gives Up on You* while doing this study, read chapters 10–12.

Day 1

SETTLING FOR SHECHEM

Although we are often encouraged not to settle for things—whether in our relationships, in our careers, in our dreams, in our goals—the truth is that we do choose to compromise. The dream job we had our sights on at age twenty-two doesn't seem practical anymore. The house we thought we would own one day is still outside our price range. The list of perfect qualities we thought we would find in a mate . . . well, we settled on a few of those items.

In life, it is inevitable that we will settle for certain things. But there's a difference between the type of settling that leads to contentment and the type that leads to "Shechem." The former is a surrender—recognizing the perfect house, mate, or job may not exist and seeing the good that God has put in front of us. The latter is a result of overt disobedience to God's plans for our lives—settling for what *we* want rather than what *he* wants.

Settling for Shechem does not bring contentment. It only brings pain and heartache. It will make us feel as if we're trapped. It will take us away from God rather than bring us closer to him. We've all been there. We've all spent time in Shechem, regretting the decisions that brought us there, and trying to pretend that everything is fine.

God did not want Jacob to settle for Shechem, and he doesn't want us to settle either. He has better plans for us. He has a blessing for us in "Bethel"—a place where we honor him, where our relationship with him is made right, and where the path before us becomes clear. It is a path that will lead us out of the shadow of Shechem and into the light.

READ | JEREMIAH 29:11–14 AND JOHN 10:7–10

REFLECT

1. Jeremiah was active as a prophet from the time of King Josiah of Judah (626 BC) until the fall of Jerusalem (587 BC). He prophesied that the people of Judah would turn from God and be taken into captivity, but in this passage, he relayed a hopeful message that the people would eventually be restored to God and to Jerusalem. What does God say his plans are for his people? What promise is given to them in this passage?

2. Jesus compared himself to a shepherd in the passage from the Gospel of John. Shepherds were known to risk their lives to protect their flocks, keeping them safe from thieves and other dangers.[10] Who or what do you think Jesus is referring to when he mentions "thieves and robbers" in this passage? What does Jesus provide instead?

3. God has plans for each of us and will lead us like a Good Shepherd into the abundant life that he has in store for us. But when are some times in your life that you instead settled for Shechem? What led you there and what kept you there?

4. Why do you think it is so easy to just settle for Shechem instead of taking the steps that God says are necessary to secure the blessing that he has for us in Bethel?

PRAY | Whether you've settled for Shechem in the past, are currently in a version of Shechem, or are thinking about going there, ask God for his guidance. It is so tempting to go our own way—to settle for what's easy or shiny or worldly—but God has a plan to prosper and bless you. Ask him to lead you to the place where you can experience the blessing of Bethel.

Day 2

A VOICE FOR THE VOICELESS

Everyone seemed to have an opinion about what should happen after Dinah, Jacob's only daughter, was raped by Shechem (same name as the city), the son of Hamor. Shechem thought Dinah should be his wife. Hamor thought this was a good idea and, while they were at it, that all of his people should intermarry with Jacob's people. Jacob's sons thought every man in Shechem should die. Jacob was worried about what it all would mean for him and his future.

It seems the one person's opinion that mattered the most—that of Dinah—goes unspoken or at least unrecorded. What was going through her mind? What did *she* think should happen? The fact that Scripture doesn't tell us isn't surprising. The voice of the victim is often the last to be heard and, even if it is, rarely believed. For Dinah in the time and culture in which she lived, her future was at the mercy of the men around her.

Perhaps you know what this feels like. To be voiceless and powerless. To not get a seat at the table or a say in the conversation. To have your fate determined by the powers around you. But it's worth noting that while Dinah's voice is not heard in Scripture, her *story* is told. The Bible doesn't ignore her tale and shy away from relating what happened to her at the hands of Shechem. We know her name because her story was *not* swept under the rug. The Bible elevates the voiceless and powerless again and again.

Jesus knew something about being powerless. He was from a small agricultural village and did not rub shoulders with the rich and powerful. In fact, the rich and powerful didn't really like him. They tried to take his voice, his power, and his life—but it couldn't be taken. Jesus was raised from the dead and, with him, every voice of the oppressed, every enslaved people group, and every victim and survivor now has ultimate victory in their Savior.

READ | LUKE 4:16–21

REFLECT

1. Jesus gave this sermon at the start of his ministry in his hometown of Nazareth. He quoted the prophet Isaiah and said that he was the fulfillment of this prophecy. For what does Jesus say he was anointed? What type of people did he come to serve?

2. Why do you think Jesus chose this passage to mark the beginning of his ministry?

3. When have you felt voiceless or powerless? What was that experience like for you?

4. When you consider the story of Dinah as related in the book of Genesis, how do you feel that the Bible treats the voiceless and powerless? What does this mean for how we should treat those around us who find themselves without a voice?

PRAY | Ask God what he is calling you to today. Could he be calling you to deeper healing from a past wound or trauma? Could he be calling you to tell your story to help others who have gone through something similar? Or could he be calling you to be a voice for the voiceless?

Day 3

LOWERING THE LADDER

God never gave up on Jacob. We wouldn't have blamed him if he did. Jacob seemed intent on going his own way, taking shortcuts, and making deals with the Lord rather than being in relationship with him. Still, God pursued Jacob. He came to him at Bethel in a dream and promised to be with him. He came to him in Paddan Aram and told him it was time to return home. He came to him again in Shechem, telling him to go to Bethel.

Not only does God refuse to give up on us but he also *pursues* us. He comes after us. He doesn't wait for us to come back to him, tapping his foot with his arms crossed. No, he speaks to us, shows us the way, and corrects our course. God does not stand on a ladder and tell us to climb it and find him. Instead, he lowers a ladder in the wilderness of our lives and finds us.

This is exactly what God did when he sent us his Son. God literally lowered himself to the status of a human being to provide a way for us out of sin and into eternal life with him. As the apostle Paul wrote, "Being found in appearance as a man, he humbled himself by becoming obedient to death—even death on a cross" (Philippians 2:8). God didn't send Jesus to us along with a long list of requirements for what we have to do to get to heaven. No, he sent Jesus and said, "This is it. This is all you need. No work or effort required. The work has been done."

If you are still living a performative faith—one in which you believe in God's grace but also feel that your salvation relies on what you do—then draw hope from Jacob's story. He hardly did *anything* right in his entire life, yet God still offered his grace to him. This is because God's grace is not about your performance but about his great love. So no more reaching. No more striving. The ladder from heaven has been lowered down to you.

READ | ROMANS 3:21–24

REFLECT

1. In this passage, the apostle Paul clearly lays out the central message of the gospel. What is that message? Why did God do this for us?

2. How did God ultimately set things right with Jacob? How does this mirror the way in which Jesus set things right for us?

3. It's one thing to cognitively believe in God's grace through Jesus. It's another to live that out as truth. Where are you on the spectrum? Have you fully accepted God's grace through Jesus, or do you still believe you need to do certain things to earn God's love? Explain your response.

4. What are some of the ways that you have witnessed God "lowering the ladder" into your life? How have you seen God pursue you and rescue you with his grace?

PRAY | Think about any ways in which you are trying to earn God's love, grace, or forgiveness. Be honest with God about this. Thank him for sending his Son so you can have full confidence in his love for you. Ask Jesus to renew your understanding of his grace and to help you let go of any earning or striving so that you can simply receive his love as a free gift.

Day 4

HE DIED WORSHIPING

It is not the beginning of a race that determines how the participants will finish. Runners might go out strong, sweeping past everyone else on the course, only to lose steam in the last mile. The opposite can also happen. Runners may not have a strong start, but somewhere in the middle they pick up the pace and cross the finish line stronger than when they started. This latter scenario seems to have been what happened in the life of our patriarch Jacob.

In Hebrews 11, the author lists hero after hero of the faith who served God. After everything you've studied about Jacob's life, you might think the author would have left him out of the chapter. After all, he was the crooked bough on the family tree. But right there, after Abraham and before Joseph, Jacob is prominently mentioned—and not for what he did *wrong* but for what he did *right*: "By faith Jacob, when he was dying, blessed each of Joseph's sons, and worshiped" (verse 21). (Read the full description of Jacob's death in Genesis 49.)

Jacob finished his race stronger than he started it. This can be true for you as well. Just because you have had a rough few miles (or years) doesn't mean it's too late to turn things around. You don't have to go down in history for the miles behind you. You can be remembered for the ones ahead. By God's grace, a life of wrong turns can be turned into a life of worship—a life that looks to God rather than yourself, that focuses on his grace rather than your flaws, and one that points others to the life-changing love of Jesus.

READ | HEBREWS 11:20–22, 32–40

REFLECT

1. Notice what Hebrews 11:21 says about Jacob. If you didn't know anything else about Jacob except what is written about him here, what kind of man would you think he was? Why do you think the author of Hebrews commemorated Jacob in this way?

2. Hebrews was written to encourage new believers to continue in the way of Christ, the new covenant, rather than return to the old covenant of their forefathers.[11] The promise the author refers to in verses 39–40 is Jesus. What does this mean in the context of Jacob's life and death? How is Jesus the "perfecter" of the patriarchs' faith?

3. Read through all the things that the author lists happened to heroes of the faith. What impressions do you get about these people when you read these descriptions?

4. If your name were to be recorded in this list of the great heroes in the Hall of Faith, how would you want to be remembered?

PRAY | Use this prayer time to reflect on what you've learned about Jacob, God, and yourself in this study. Thank God for the insights he has given you through his Word. Also thank him for never giving up on you.

Day 5
WRAP IT UP

Use this time to go back and complete any of the study and reflection questions from previous days that you weren't able to finish. Make note of what God has revealed to you in these days. Finally, talk with your group about what study you may want to go through next. Put a date on the calendar for when you'll meet next to study God's Word and dive deeper into community.

LEADER'S GUIDE

Thank you for your willingness to lead your group through this study! What you have chosen to do is valuable and will make a great difference in the lives of others. *God Never Gives Up on You* is a five-session Bible study built around video content and small-group interaction. As the group leader, imagine yourself as the host of a party. Your job is to take care of your guests by managing the details so that when your guests arrive, they can focus on one another and on the interaction around the topic for that session.

Your role as the group leader is not to answer all the questions or reteach the content—the video, book, and study guide will do most of that work. Your job is to guide the experience and cultivate your small group into a connected and engaged community. This will make it a place for members to process, question, and reflect—not necessarily receive more instruction.

There are several elements in this leader's guide that will help you as you structure your study and reflection time, so be sure to follow along and take advantage of each one.

Before You Begin

Before your first meeting, make sure the group members have a copy of this study guide. Alternatively, you can hand out the study guides at your first meeting and give the members some time to look over the material and ask any preliminary questions. Also make sure they are aware that they have access to the streaming videos at any time. During your first meeting, ask the members to provide their name, phone number, and email address so you can keep in touch with them.

Generally, the ideal size for a group is eight to ten people, which will ensure that everyone has enough time to participate in discussions. If you have more people, you might want to break up the main group into smaller subgroups. Encourage those who show up at the first meeting to commit to attending the duration of the study, as this will help the group members get to know one another, create stability for the group, and help you know how to best prepare to lead them through the material.

Each of the sessions begins with an opening reflection in the Welcome section. The questions that follow in the Connect section serve as an icebreaker to get the group members thinking about the topic. Some people may want to tell a long story in response to one of these questions, but the goal is to keep the answers brief. Ideally, you want everyone in the group to get a chance to answer, so try to keep the responses to a minute or less. If you have talkative group members, say up front that everyone needs to limit their answer to one minute.

Give the group members a chance to answer, but also tell them to feel free to pass if they wish. With the rest of the study, it's generally not a good idea to have everyone answer every question—a free-flowing discussion is more desirable. But with the opening icebreaker questions, you can go around the circle. Encourage shy people to share, but don't force them.

At your first meeting, let the group members know that each session contains a personal study section they can use to continue to engage with the content until the next meeting. While this is optional, it will help them cement the concepts presented during the group study time and help them better understand the story of Jacob. Let them know that if they choose to do so, they can watch the video for the next session by accessing the streaming code. Invite them to bring any questions and insights to your next meeting, especially if they had a breakthrough moment or didn't understand something.

PREPARATION FOR EACH SESSION

As the leader, there are a few things you should do to prepare for each meeting:

- **Read through the session.** This will help you become more familiar with the content and know how to structure the discussion times.

- **Decide how the videos will be used.** Determine whether you want the members to watch the videos ahead of time (again, via the streaming access code) or together as a group.

- **Decide which questions you want to discuss.** Based on the length of your group discussions, you may not be able to get through all the questions. So look over the recommendations for the suggested and additional questions in each session and choose which ones you definitely want to cover.

- **Be familiar with the questions you want to discuss.** When the group meets, you'll be watching the clock, so make sure you are familiar with the questions that you have selected. In this way, you will ensure that you have the material more deeply in your mind than your group members.

- **Pray for your group.** Pray for your group members and ask God to lead them as they study his Word.

In many cases, there will be no one "right" answer to the question. Answers will vary, especially when the group members are being asked to share their personal experiences.

STRUCTURING THE DISCUSSION TIME

You will need to determine with your group how long you want to meet so you can plan your time accordingly. Suggested times for each section have been provided in this study guide, and if you adhere to these times, your group will meet for ninety minutes, as noted below. If you want to meet for two hours, follow the times given in the right-hand column:

Section	90 Minutes	120 Minutes
CONNECT (discuss one or more of the opening questions for the session)	15 minutes	20 minutes
WATCH (watch the teaching material together and take notes)	20 minutes	20 minutes
DISCUSS (discuss the study questions you selected ahead of time)	35 minutes	50 minutes
RESPOND (write down key takeaways)	10 minutes	15 minutes
PRAY (pray together and dismiss)	10 minutes	15 minutes

As the group leader, it is up to you to keep track of the time and keep things on schedule. You might want to set a timer for each segment so both you and the group members know when your time is up. Don't be concerned if the group members are quiet or slow to share. People are often quiet when they are pulling together their ideas, and this might be a new experience for them. Just ask a question and then let it hang in the air for a while until someone shares. You can then say, "Thank you. What about others? What came to you when you watched that portion of the teaching?"

GROUP DYNAMICS

Leading a group through *God Never Gives Up on You* will prove to be highly rewarding both to you and your group members. But you still may encounter challenges along the way! Discussions can get off track. Group members may not be sensitive to the needs and ideas of others. Some might worry they will be expected to talk about matters that make them feel awkward. Others may express comments that result in disagreements. To help ease this strain on you and the group, consider the following ground rules:

- When someone raises a question or comment that is off the main topic, suggest that you deal with it another time, or, if you feel led to go in that direction, let the group know you will be spending some time discussing it.

- If someone asks a question that you don't know how to answer, admit it and move on. At your discretion, feel free to invite group members to comment on questions that call for personal experience.

- If you find one or two people are dominating the discussion time, direct a few questions to others in the group. Outside the main group time, ask the more dominating members to help you draw out the quieter ones. Work to make them a part of the solution instead of part of the problem.

- When a disagreement occurs, encourage the group members to process the matter in love. Encourage those on opposite sides to restate what they heard the other side say about the matter, and then invite each side to evaluate if that perception is accurate. Lead the group in examining other scriptures related to the topic and look for common ground.

When any of these issues arise, encourage your group members to follow these words from Scripture: "Love one another" (John 13:34); "If it is possible, as far as it depends on you, live at peace with everyone" (Romans 12:18); and "Be quick to listen, slow to speak and slow to become angry" (James 1:19).

Thank you again for taking the time to lead your group. You are making a difference in your group members' lives and having an impact as they learn from the story of Jacob's life about what it means that God never gives up on them.

ABOUT THE AUTHOR

Since entering the ministry in 1978, Max Lucado has served churches in Miami, Florida; Rio de Janeiro, Brazil; and San Antonio, Texas. He currently serves as Teaching Minister of Oak Hills Church in San Antonio. He is the recipient of the 2021 ECPA Pinnacle Award for his outstanding contribution to the publishing industry and society at large. He is America's bestselling inspirational author with more than 145 million books in print.

ENDNOTES

1. John H. Walton, Victor H. Matthews, and Mark W. Chavalas, *The IVP Bible Background Commentary: Old Testament* (Downers Grove, IL: InterVarsity Press, 2000), 48.
2. Wayne McCown, *Asbury Bible Commentary* (Grand Rapids, MI: Zondervan, 1992).
3. "What Is Healthy Soil?" UC Marin Master Gardeners, University of California Agriculture and Natural Resources, https://marinmg.ucanr.edu/BASICS/SOIL_813/What_Is_Healthy_Soil/.
4. Walton, Matthews, and Chavalas, *IVP Bible Background Commentary: Old Testament*, 262.
5. Walton, Matthews, and Chavalas, *IVP Bible Background Commentary: Old Testament*, 262.
6. Charles R. Swindoll, *So, You Want to Be like Christ? Eight Essentials to Get You There* (Nashville, TN: Thomas Nelson, 2007).
7. Walton, Matthews, and Chavalas, *IVP Bible Background Commentary: Old Testament*, 62.
8. St. John of the Cross, "The Dark Night of the Soul," Poetry Foundation, accessed April 25, 2023, https://www.poetryfoundation.org/poems/157984/the-dark-night-of-the-soul.
9. Eugene H. Peterson, *Five Smooth Stones for Pastoral Work* (United Kingdom: Eerdmans, 1992), 49.
10. Craig S. Keener, *The IVP Bible Background Commentary: New Testament* (Downers Grove, IL: InterVarsity Press, 1993), 290.
11. "Receiving the Promise," Ligonier Ministries, October 18, 2004, https://www.ligonier.org/learn/devotionals/receiving-promise.

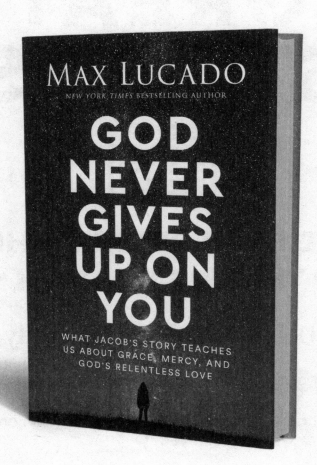

From the Publisher

GREAT STUDIES

ARE EVEN BETTER WHEN THEY'RE SHARED!

Help others find this study:

- Post a review at your favorite online bookseller.

- Post a picture on a social media account and share why you enjoyed it.

- Send a note to a friend who would also love it—or, better yet, go through it with them!

Thanks for helping others grow their faith!